Advance Praise for
The Capitalism Paradox

"Political economy in its finest explores the institutional arrangement that promotes productive specialization and peaceful social coopera- tion. Paul Rubin's *The Capitalism Paradox* is an outstanding corrective to mischaracterization and misunderstanding of political economy, often perpetuated by economists themselves. At the foundation of our understanding and appreciation of the market economy must be this recognition of how trade and commerce in general reinforces human sociability and social cooperation. The market is a positive sum game of wealth creation through human cooperation. Brilliant, concise, and to the point, Rubin's work should be read by all students of society."

—PETER BOETTKE, University Professor of Economics and Philosophy,
George Mason University

"In this wonderful book, Paul Rubin gently takes economists to task for talking about competition as if it is the engine of markets and the econ- omy and forgetting that cooperation is the real engine. He concisely and persuasively reminds economists that market transactions make both parties happy, not one a winner and the other a loser, and argues for new ways of explaining economics in that light."

—DR. ADRIAN MOORE, Vice President, Reason Foundation

"Speaking is natural to humans while reading must be taught. Accord- ing to Paul Rubin, politics (and its zero-sum view of the world) is also natural while economics (and its positive-sum view of the world) must be taught because humans evolved when life was zero-sum. There is no better way for someone to learn an appreciation for markets, econom- ics, and the positive-sum nature of modern life than to read this book by Professor Rubin."

—PETER VAN DOREN, Senior Fellow, Cato Institute and Editor,
Regulation Magazine

Paul Rubin

THE CAPITALISM PARADOX

THE
CAPITALISM
PARADOX

HOW COOPERATION ENABLES
FREE MARKET COMPETITION

PAUL H. RUBIN

PostHill
PRESS

A BOMBARDIER BOOKS BOOK
An Imprint of Post Hill Press

The Capitalism Paradox:
How Cooperation Enables Free Market Competition
© 2019 by Paul H. Rubin
All Rights Reserved

ISBN: 978-1-64293-139-6
ISBN (eBook): 978-1-64293-140-2

Cover photo image: Created by Jcomp–Freepik.com, "image: Freepik.com."
This cover has been designed using resources from Freepik.com
Cover design by Abby Adelman
Author photo by Barbara Banks Photography
Interior design and composition by Greg Johnson, Textbook Perfect

Post Hill Press
New York • Nashville
posthillpress.com

Published in the United States of America

To Martie Moss,
my exceptional and beautiful wife,
who has always encouraged
and supported my work.

CONTENTS

INTRODUCTION

Economists are the most important advocates of free markets (In a free market economy, property rights are well defined and there is minimal government intervention). The Reagan administration was famous for supporting markets. But even so, when I was in president Ronald Reagan's Council of Economic Advisers, I found that we economists were the major believers in markets. Others supported us in defending markets when various pro-business or deficit-limiting policies were involved, but the CEA was the only entity that actually supported markets and market freedom under all circumstances.

But even though we economists are the major supporters of markets, in some cases we actually sabotage them. This is not intentional; we think we are supporting markets, and we often are. But our language often serves to turn people away from markets, and acts to generate hostility. In particular, our use of the term "competition" and our love of "competitive markets" often serves to disguise the true nature of markets, and to turn people away from the markets and from economics. In fact, markets are much more cooperative than they are competitive, and if we emphasized this more, then people would better understand the benefits of free exchange. We economists make our living by providing advice about the economy, but one purpose of this book is to provide advice to my fellow economists in order to make our advocacy more effective.

This book aims to explain and clarify this argument. In doing so, I make several interrelated points. First, markets are the most efficient institution for running an economy, and the more an economy relies on markets, the higher the level of happiness, health, and wealth. Second, many people do not understand markets or the benefits they provide. Third, people have no intuitive understanding of economics or how an economy functions. Fourth, one reason why people may not like markets is because they view markets as being "competitive," and many people do not like competition because they associate competition with a chance of losing. Those who view the world as competitive are more likely to dislike markets. Fifth, markets are actually more cooperative than they are competitive, and we economists have erred by emphasizing the competitive aspect of markets while ignoring or downplaying the cooperative aspect. Finally, there is an important role for competition, but competition is subordinate to cooperation in an economy. Cooperation is the "main event" and competition is the opener.

Benefits of Markets

Markets are truly amazing institutions. Market economies have generated tremendous benefits for mankind. Markets by far provide more benefits than any other form of economic organization. We can see this at whatever level we look: globally, between countries, and even within countries.

At the global level, the results of the most important social science experiment in history are in. The Soviet Union, the largest attempt at a nonmarket economy, has collapsed. The market economies of the West have survived and thrived, albeit with some rocky patches.

We also have evidence from smaller experiments. Both Korea and Germany have been divided into market and nonmarket segments. In both cases, the market economies (South Korea, West Germany) have done extremely well, and the nonmarket segments have either collapsed (East Germany) or are providing extreme misery for their residents (North Korea). More recently, Venezuela has replaced a market economy with a centrally planned economy and has gone from prosperity to chaos, hyperinflation (1 million percent per year), dictatorship, and starvation.

At a more detailed level, there is pervasive evidence that more free market economies work better than less free economies. Students of economic freedom say that freedom exists when (1) property acquired without the use of force, fraud, or theft is protected from physical invasions by others, and (2) individuals are free to use, exchange, or give their property to another as long as their actions do not violate the identical rights of others. This leads to five components of economic freedom:

- The size of government: government spending, taxes, and government enterprises are limited.
- Property rights are protected from government and from private predators, and there is rule of law and freedom of contract.
- Sound money policies lead to limited and moderate inflation.
- International trade and trade policies allow free trade.
- Regulation of business, labor, and credit markets is limited.

The intuition behind the value of each of these measures is clear. Without enforceable property rights, others can steal your property or government can confiscate it, which are clearly not conducive to freedom. Having few market regulations and being able to trade with international partners are direct examples of economic freedom. The size of government might be a less obvious measure, but when government is large, economic freedom is low because mandatory taxes and government spending supplant personal choice. Lastly, sound monetary policy is needed to prevent any gains of trade from being dissipated by the unstable value of money and actions people adopt to protect the value of their assets.

With respect to the above five components of economic freedom, economists invariably find a positive correlation between economic freedom and economic growth. Freer economies grow more quickly. Estimates of the correlation (statistical relationship, ranging from -1 to +1) between economic freedom and growth generally range from +0.20 to +0.40, and every estimate is statistically positive and significantly different from zero. This large, positive correlation indicates that freedom is directly associated with growth: more freedom, more growth. The overall effect of freedom on growth comes both from direct and indirect effects.

Freedom works directly to increase growth, as people are better able to use resources efficiently in a freer economy. Conversely, government regulation can hamper growth by preventing people from using resources efficiently. As an example, the World Bank estimates that, in the United States, it takes five days to start a new business at a cost equal to 1.5 percent of income per capita. In Bolivia, it takes forty-nine days at a cost of 71.6 percent of income per capita. Facing higher startup costs, fewer Bolivian citizens will open businesses. They will not enter what could otherwise be profitable opportunities and will not provide desired goods and services to consumers. This lower regulatory cost of business formation, along with many regulatory cost differences, is a major reason why the U.S. has a healthier and richer economy than Bolivia.

Regulation can also mandate inefficient resource use. Sometimes governments grant monopolies to select individuals, thereby denying others the right to trade at all. If a government grants a monopoly on taxi cabs to an inept company, then people might waste time waiting for cabs because too few drivers are employed, or they might be late to important events because drivers are unreliable, or they may not travel because monopolized taxicabs are more expensive than freer taxicabs. Even if the monopoly is given to the very best company, some people might prefer would-be competitors. Not everyone wants to pay a high price for good service. Some would rather pay a lower price for less reliable service. With a government-enforced monopoly, however, this choice is made for them.

Even regulation that is seemingly "good" can also lead to inefficient resource use. The minimum wage is often justified as needed to protect workers. Without the minimum wage, employers might pay wages that some consider "too low." Of course, employers would only pay those wages if employees were willing to accept them. Without a minimum wage law, employers might have found it profitable to hire an employee at a wage below the minimum wage. With a minimum wage law, the employee may not be hired at all; the actual "minimum wage" is always zero. If the employee would have been willing to accept the below-minimum wage, but instead is unemployed, people suffer losses in self-esteem and lack of training, and resources are going to waste. The potential employer and employee are not permitted to enter a productive relationship. In all of these examples, regulation is stopping the mutually beneficial trade that a freer society would permit.

Freedom also works indirectly. Freedom leads to more investment in both physical capital (machines, factories, buildings) and human capital (training and education), and this increased investment also leads to increased growth. For example, if property rights are well protected, then people are more willing to invest because their investment is more secure. If there is less occupational regulation, workers have more freedom to get training in jobs that interest them or that pay well, and so there will be more human capital investment. If taxes are low, then both kinds of investment pay more, and hard work also pays more. For all these reasons and many more, increased freedom of markets leads to increased wealth. These results apply both across countries and across states in the U.S.

Figure 1 on page 6 shows the average income per capita for countries ranked by their measure of economic freedom. The average income of the freest 25 percent of countries is nearly two times that of the next 25 percent of countries and *over six times* that of the least free countries. Given the small size of the incomes in the poorest countries and the cost of expensive services like health care and education, this gap entails a huge loss of human well-being.

Even within countries, differences in economic freedom matter. Figure 2 shows the same thing as Figure 1 but with states in the U.S. The picture is not as stark, but the story remains the same. Residents of the freest 25 percent of states earn almost $5,000 more per year than residents of the least free states. States that might otherwise look similar can perform quite differently. Relatively freer Alabama has higher per capita income than relatively unfree Mississippi ($4,400 more per year); likewise for New Hampshire and Vermont ($5,700 more per year).

The numbers only tell part of the story. It is virtually impossible to understand what life would be like without the benefits created by capitalism and free markets. To make the issues concrete, consider a

Figure 1. Ecomomic Freedom at the Country Level and Income Per Capita, 2012

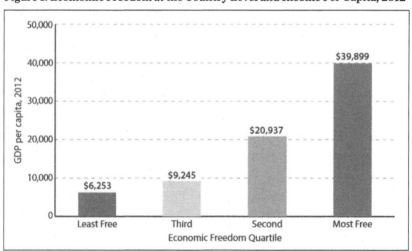

Source: Economic Freedom of the World Index, 2014

Figure 2. USA Economic Freedom at the State Level and GDP Per Capita, 2011

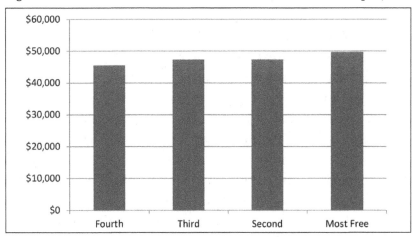

Source: Economic Freedom of the World Index, 2013. The "Subnational" index is used (measured in 2011 U.S. Dollars)

contemporary person—say, a college student named Bennie getting ready to go to a Bernie Sanders pro-socialism rally.

First, there is only about a 50 percent chance that Bennie would even be alive. Child mortality was on the order of 50 percent before the invention of modern drugs, clean water, and other benefits provided by capitalism. (Clean water is often supplied by governments but paid for by using the wealth generated by capitalism.) Drugs and medical care are provided by capitalists seeking a profit, and hospitals are financed by the wealth generated by capitalism, either through charity of the wealthy or by taxes.

Second, Bennie, if he had survived, would almost certainly not be a college student. College is an investment in that Bennie forgoes earning income during a lengthy period of education. But wealth is needed to finance this period of zero earnings, and this wealth can only exist in a capitalist economy. The cost of education may be paid by Bennie's parents or by the state, as in a public institution, or by Bennie himself through borrowing. But in any case, someone must pay for the investment, and this can only be possible in a wealthy economy. Wealth is needed to finance the physical buildings, the professors' salaries, and Bennie's consumption during the period of education. Although some higher education existed before capitalism, it was uncommon.

Third, consider the process of the rally. Bennie probably first learned about Bernie Sanders on his computer (produced by a capitalist firm) over the internet (run by capitalist firms). He learned about the time and place of the protest on his smartphone, again the product of capitalism. He drove there in his car, which runs on gasoline, on roads financed by government using taxes on capitalist wealth.

I need not go on. Anyone can read a history or anthropology book and learn about life before (without) capitalism. It is absurd and bizarre to advocate elimination of capitalism. If a society becomes socialist, it can function for a while by living off of the capital produced when the economy was free, but eventually it will run out. Soviet Russia lasted about seventy years, in part because it removed huge amounts of capital from Germany after World War II.

This forecast of doom may seem fanciful. But we need look no farther than Venezuela to see the actual occurrence of social collapse caused by replacing capitalism with socialism. Venezuela replaced a thriving market economy with a socialist economy and is now a complete economic, social, and political disaster, with widespread hunger, shortages, and emigration, with inflation of 1 million percent per year, and with a corrupt dictator. Indeed, it is puzzling how so many can desire "democratic" or any other form of socialism, with Venezuela as a contemporary example of the effects. Perhaps it is because the media, in describing the disaster that is Venezuela, generally does not mention that socialism has been the cause.

The collapse of Venezuela was quite rapid. Hugo Chávez was first elected in 1998, and the collapse was in full force by 2015 and perhaps sooner. The U.S. could last longer, but if we really went to full socialism we would ultimately collapse as well.

The U.S. Council of Economic Advisers (2018) recently estimated the costs of various movements toward socialism in the U.S. If we were to adopt "Medicare for All," a centralized socialized medical system, the costs would be 9 percent of gross domestic product, or about $7,000 per person in 2022, due to high tax rates that would reduce incentives. Other socialist-type policies would reduce income by even more. A Venezuela-type economic reorganization would reduce GDP by about 40 percent, or $24,000 per capita. If we were to adopt Nordic-type labor regulations, GDP would fall by $2,000 to $5,000 per year. If we adopted the more socialistic polices of the Nordic countries in the 1970s, GDP would fall by 19 percent, or $11,000 per capita. There is no free lunch, and socialistic policies are a very expensive dinner.

In addition to the economic benefits of free markets, there are terrible human costs of sufficiently unfree societies. The limit of unfreedom is Communism. The best estimate is that in the twentieth century, communist regimes killed about one hundred million people: Russia, twenty million; China sixty-five million; and the rest in a miscellany of countries including Vietnam, Cambodia, North Korea, and others (Courtois, 2017). Because Communism denies people the freedom they desire, the only way it can maintain itself is through force, which is why it has led to so many deaths. This makes it even more surprising that so many are apparently in favor of returning to this horrible episode in human history.

Emporiophobia: Fear of Markets

Clearly, economic freedom has a steady and strong link to economic welfare. Given this link, there is a major puzzle: Why do so many people reject economic freedom and markets? Evidence that people are hostile toward markets is all around us. For example, the U.S. has recently twice elected an administration that increased the level of regulation of markets and attempted to replace a major segment of the economy, the health care segment, with a nonmarket institution.

President Donald Trump was elected largely on a platform of anti-market rhetoric in the form of restricting immigration and reducing imports, although in practice he has increased market freedom in many dimensions. Many voters preferred Bernie Sanders, an avowed socialist. England in the 1950s moved away from a market economy, and it was only with a great deal of effort that Margaret Thatcher could move it back toward a market economy, and even today many resent this move. France recently elected a socialist government. Argentina was a thriving market economy in the 1930s and early 1940s, but beginning in 1945 elected a nonmarket government. (More recently it is returning to prosperity under a more market-oriented regime.) China is an odd economy but is at least in part communist, as are Cuba and North Korea.

There are also particular segments of societies that reject markets. These include the media, intellectuals in general (Sowell, 2011), and many Jews. All of these groups have thrived under markets. For example, intellectuals need funding, and capitalist economies generate the wealth needed for intellectual activity. The great economist Milton Friedman (himself Jewish, as am I) pointed out that Jews have everywhere thrived as participants in markets, and yet their voting behavior is commonly anti-market (Friedman, 1972/1988). Thus, it is not obvious why so many of them reject markets. Since Friedman's argument, Israel has moved much closer to a market economy and is thriving.

At American universities (the richest in the world because of the wealth generated by capitalist markets) to call someone a capitalist is almost an insult. Many intellectuals in some disciplines are still Marxists, despite the evidence of the fall of the Soviet Union and the chaos of Venezuela. For example, in the humanities much analysis is in terms of "race, class, and gender," a thinly disguised version of Marxism, the major anti-market philosophy of our time. Bernie Sanders ran as a socialist and got much of the Democratic vote, and even now a majority of young people reject capitalism; a recent Harvard Poll

(Harvard Youth Poll, July 2016) found that 51 percent of millennials rejected capitalism. A 2016 poll by YouGov found that favorable views of capitalism were 47 percent among Generation Z, 42 percent among Millennials, and 45 percent among Generation X (YouGov, 2016). There are other results in this poll indicating that younger people are relatively less favorable toward capitalism and relatively more favorable toward socialism or communism. A recent poll has found that 51 percent of Democrats, 26 percent of independents, and 21 percent of Republicans (!) have a favorable view of socialism (Rasmussen, 2018). A more recent poll has found that more Democrats (57 percent) view socialism favorably than view capitalism favorably. In a recent election for Congress in New York City, Alexandria Ocasio-Cortez, an avowed "Democratic" socialist, won an upset victory, and she is currently a heroine of the Democratic Party. Bill de Blasio, the mayor of New York, the center of American capitalism, has recently complained that "private property rights" limit his ability to plan for New York, and he has nonetheless won a second term.

Many religions also reject aspects of markets. Capital markets are the most disliked. For example, both Christianity and Islam forbid the charging of interest on capital, and Judaism restricts it. Jesus driving the money changers from the Temple is a strongly anti-market move. The money changers were providing a useful market service: they were changing many currencies into shekels, which were needed for purchase of sacrificial animals, and Jesus' attack was a strong anti-market act. Jesus' statement that "It is easier for a camel to go through the eye of a needle than for a rich man to enter the kingdom of God" (Matthew 19, 24) is also an anti-market statement since generally the best way to become rich is through markets. In Islam, charging of interest is still banned, and capital markets are therefore opaque and inefficient as participants seek convoluted methods of actually charging and paying interest without calling it interest. The unwillingness to use interest rates as a tool is leading to instability in Turkey.

(Christianity and Judaism have managed to eliminate their prohibitions on interest.)

Religion aside, much basic market activity is still considered immoral in modern times. A clear example is the portrayal of businesspeople in the media, which is overwhelmingly negative. In movies and television, businesspeople are commonly seen as immoral and heartless. They commit criminal acts, and their businesses are rarely seen as producing anything of social value. Think of Gordon Gekko in *Wall Street* as a classic example (Ribstein, 2012; Shugan, 2006).

When people are asked about markets, especially international markets, they often react with hostility. In a recent Pew Research Center survey on global attitudes toward trade, 68 percent of Americans held that view that growing trade and business ties with other countries was a good thing. While the majority did favor international markets, this percentage means that nearly one-third of Americans *do not* hold the view that growing trade with other countries is a good thing. Furthermore, just 20 percent said that trade creates jobs. Without some basic aversion to markets, it is hard to understand why having more trading partners would be a bad thing, or why it would fail to create jobs.

Given the evidence on the benefits of capitalism and the costs of socialism, how is it that rational people can favor the latter? An important cause is limited knowledge. Many citizens of American and Western Europe do not understand the amount of wealth created by capitalism, and the poverty created by true socialism. For example, consider the statement by Alexandra Ocasio-Cortez, the elected Congresswoman, who ran as a "democratic" socialist: "Capitalism has not always existed in the world and will not always exist in the world" (PBS Interview, July 16, 2018). It is true that capitalism has not always existed, but neither has wealth. Pre-capitalist societies were vastly—to many, inconceivably—poorer than contemporary European or American societies. The natural state of humanity, through most of our existence, is what we would now call poverty. But most of us have not seen this, nor do many understand it. This is especially true in a world of zero-sum thinking.

Many people ask about the "causes of poverty." (There are about fifteen million references to this term in quotation marks on Google.) But this is a meaningless question. The natural state of humanity, throughout almost all of our existence, has been what is now called poverty. It is only since the industrial revolution, beginning in about 1760, that any significant number of people have left poverty. The industrial revolution itself was caused by well-defined property rights (including intellectual property rights) and free markets—that is, by capitalism.

Competition and Dislike of Markets

There are many reasons for this dislike or fear of markets, and entire books have been written about various aspects of this issue. I do not have a comprehensive theory. However, I do have a partial explanation, consistent with recent research by psychologists.

We have various names for a market economy: capitalist, free market, competitive. I want to focus on one: a "competitive" economy. This term is frequently used: Google indicates that there are 51 million uses of the term "competitive market economy." Moreover, a search of leading economics textbooks indicates that "competition" and its variants is used about eight times as often as "cooperative" and its variants.

I want to argue that the use of the term "competitive" to describe an economy is both inappropriate and harmful. The term "competition" in economics was borrowed from sports without much thought (Stigler, 1957). However, the use of this term in economics is inappropriate. An important theme of this book is that a market economy is much more cooperative than it is competitive. Essentially, economists use "competition" as a term of art—the word as used by economists has a special meaning. We do not mean the same thing by competition as the normal usage of the term. (Chapter 4 has a discussion of the way in which economists use the term, but the point is that as economists use the term, a competitive economy has certain highly beneficial features.) But the word "competition" also has a meaning in everyday usage, and when people other than economists hear the term, they think about the everyday meaning. This confusion is the source of much mischief.

A recent important book by two social psychologists who study the public understanding of economics and the basis for economic beliefs has a long discussion of people's views of capitalism. They find that there are many people with a deep dislike of capitalism, and many who favor it. The former includes the group of supporters of market socialism, and among the latter are, of course, most economists. They find pervasive differences between supporters and critics in many related dimensions, such as the desire for equality, the belief in the importance of individual control (pro-capitalists) versus control by outside forces, and general political conservatism versus liberalism. (In earlier research, Jim Kau and I also found persuasive and consistent sets of beliefs in voting behavior between liberals and conservatives: Kau and Rubin, 1979.) "A central feature of these models [of economic ideology] is the degree to which the social world is perceived to be essentially competitive versus cooperative in nature. In one extreme, the world is construed as a competitive jungle.... On the other pole is the view of the world as a place of cooperative harmony..." (Leiser and Shemesh, 2018, p. 85). Those who view the world as competitive are pro-capitalist. But if we could convince people that the market is also cooperative, perhaps some of those who are now anti-capitalist would begin to understand the benefits of the free market. The current emphasis by economists on competition may then lead those with a cooperative view of the world to turn away from the market economy.

I have examined the usage of the word "competition" using Google. Here are some common modifiers of "competition" and the number of Google references to each: "Cutthroat competition" (256,000), "excessive competition" (159,000), "destructive competition" (105,000), "ruthless competition" (102,000), "ferocious competition" (66,700), "vicious competition" (53,500), "unfettered competition" (37,000), "unrestrained competition" (34,500), "harmful competition" (18,000), and "dog-eat-dog competition" (15, 000). Conversely, for "beneficial competition" there are 16,400 references. For "beneficial cooperation" there are 548,000 references, and almost no references to any of the negative modifiers of cooperation. Thus, people have no difficulty in thinking of negative connotations of "competition" and are less inclined to think of competition than of cooperation as beneficial.

Although I develop this theme at length, three points will help clarify the analysis. First, the term "competition" implies a winner and a loser, but in a market both participants (buyers and sellers) gain. Second, the fundamental unit of an economic relationship is a transaction, and because both parties gain from a transaction, it is cooperative. Third, competition has an important role in a market, but its role is to ensure that transactions (cooperation) occur on the best possible terms with the best possible agents.

Moreover, even where there is competition, it is generally competition for the right to cooperate. Consider two firms engaged in active competition. For a concrete example, consider Verizon and AT&T competing for mobile phone customers based on which firm has the better network. What is the object of this competition? The object is to sign up customers—to engage in cooperation with consumers. Who will consumers choose to cooperate with? That is, which firm will get the business? The firm which can convince consumers that it offers the best combination of price, network strength, and phones. The most successful firm will be the firm that offers the best terms for cooperating with customers.

The problem with the term "competition" is that people internalize the nature of sports competition and apply it wrongly to the economy. In the world of competitive sports, there are winners and losers. A runner only wins the race because another one loses. In football, one team only gains yardage because the other team loses it. Each competitor, whether individual or team, gains only at the expense of the other competitor. In economics, this type of situation is called a "zero-sum game" because if you add the gains of one person to the losses of another, the net outcome is zero. The danger in the term "competitive market" is that people see the sports metaphor and think the economy is a zero-sum environment. In reality, nothing could be further from the truth.

When two people voluntarily trade a good or service, they only choose to do so because they both benefit from the transaction. If you offer to walk my dog for a slice of my famous chocolate cake, and I accept, then we only complete the deal because I prefer having you walk the dog to having the slice of cake, and you would rather walk the dog than miss out on the cake. Trade is emphatically not a zero-sum game. Both parties benefit from it. Of course, the number of available goods and services and the number of market participants is far too large to trade them directly. It would take too long to find people interested in direct barter. Maybe you are allergic to chocolate but would like a Danish, which I don't know how to make, in which case we would have to seek out other interested parties. Fortunately, money was created as a medium of exchange. Unfortunately, while the use of money greatly facilitates trade, it also contributes to wrongful zero-sum thinking about the economy.

When people see wealth and poverty, they often drift into zero-sum thinking. If I sell you an item, I have five dollars more, but you have five dollars less. In terms of only money, buying and selling appears to be zero-sum. If the world is zero-sum, then it must be that some people are rich because they have taken money from the poor. But this line of thinking ignores the fact that voluntary trade benefits both parties. Money *only* changes hands because parties mutually benefit from some type of exchange. The rich are rich because they have produced something that others value, and the poor are poor because they have little to sell.

Incorrect zero-sum thinking contributes directly to hostility toward markets. For example, in a survey of the American public and economists, the public strongly believes that the economy is not doing as well as it could be because "business profits are too high." But how can business profits be too high? Surely the economy does not suffer from businesses providing too many services to consumers at prices they are willing to pay. Profits, if they are legitimately obtained, are a sign that beneficial exchange is occurring. Certainly, they are not a reason for the economy performing badly.

Given that markets create so many benefits, it is perhaps surprising that so many people exhibit such a fear or dislike of them. Markets do not always function perfectly, which could explain part of the aversion, but, importantly, fear of markets goes much deeper than a recognition of the few cases where they do not work well. Emporiophobia (fear of the market) is interfering negatively and harmfully with markets across the globe. Understanding the origins of emporiophobia, even just some of them, could have an enormous impact on human welfare if it leads to people overcoming that fear.

Although this book is nontechnical—it avoids technical language and mathematics—and written for a general audience, I hope my fellow economists will absorb its lessons. In particular, I hope that we economists can begin focusing our discussions on the cooperative nature of a modern economy. My deeper hope is that a change in language to a more accurate description of the economy will do something to reduce people's misunderstanding and dislike of markets.

What Do Economists Know?

There are some truths that are basic to economics but that are nonintuitive. If these issues were more widely understood, then markets would be viewed more favorably. It is these basic truths that I want to concentrate on.

The most basic premise of economics—which is totally nonintuitive—is that hundreds of millions of people can interact with one another with no central direction and no coordination, and yet can reach a consistent outcome which itself has certain nice properties. This is Adam Smith's famous "invisible hand." Because this is not understood, there are frequent calls for central direction and central planning, despite their massive failure in the Soviet Union and wherever else they have been tried.

The second thing that economists know is that selfish behavior can nonetheless lead to desirable outcomes. The uncoordinated behavior can be motivated by selfish ends, and yet the outcome will generally be efficient. Motives do not matter; outcomes matter.

A third thing economists know that is nonintuitive is that the world is not zero-sum. Economies can grow, and it is possible for the rich to get richer at the same time that the poor get richer. The common homily "The rich get richer and the poor get poorer" is neither certain nor sure; it is totally contrary to fact in a growing market economy.

Anti-Market Quotes

Before providing the main arguments, I provide a small sample of quotations from people hostile to markets.

> *"Capitalism is a system in which the central institutions of society are in principle under autocratic control. Thus, a corporation or an industry is, if we were to think of it in political terms, fascist; that is, it has tight control at the top and strict obedience has to be established at every level—there's a little bargaining, a little give and take, but the line of authority is perfectly straightforward. Just as I'm opposed to political fascism, I'm opposed to economic fascism. I think that until major institutions of society are under the popular control of participants and communities, it's pointless to talk about democracy.*
>
> *"In this sense, I would describe myself as a libertarian socialist— I'd love to see centralized power eliminated, whether it's the state or*

the economy, and have it diffused and ultimately under direct control of the participants. Moreover, I think that's entirely realistic. Every bit of evidence that exists (there isn't much) seems to show, for example, that workers' control increases efficiency. Nevertheless, capitalists don't want it, naturally; what they're worried about is control, not the loss of productivity or efficiency."

—NOAM CHOMSKY, *Chomsky on Democracy and Education*, Psychology Press (2003)

"Modern science will continue to be blindly destructive as long as its operations are determined by the anarchism of market economic forces. The problem to be solved is whether science, technology, and industry can be brought under genuinely democratic control in the context of a global planned economy, so that all of us can collectively put our hard-won scientific knowledge to mutually beneficial use."

—CLIFFORD D. CONNER, *A People's History of Science*, Nation Books (2005)

"Capitalism places every man in competition with his fellows for a share of the available wealth. A few people accumulate big piles, but most do not. The sense of community falls victim to this struggle."

—DONALD BARTHELME, "The Rise of Capitalism" in *Sixty Stories*, Penguin (2003)

"The forces of a capitalist society, if left unchecked, tend to make the rich richer and the poor poorer."

—JAWAHARLAL NEHRU (first prime minister of India), *The New York Times Magazine* (September 7, 1958)

"[T]here is no social theory on earth short of the divine right of kings that can justify a five-hundred-fold [income] gap between management and labor."

—THOMAS FRANK, *One Market Under God*, Anchor (2001)

"Capitalism is an evil, and you cannot regulate evil. You have to eliminate it and replace it with something that is good for all people and that something is democracy."

  —MICHAEL MOORE in the movie *Capitalism: A Love Story* (2009)

"They neglect their own children so that the children of others will be cared for; they live in substandard housing so that other homes will be shiny and perfect; they endure privation so that inflation will be low and stock prices high. To be a member of the working poor is to be an anonymous donor, a nameless benefactor, to everyone."

  —BARBARA EHRENREICH, *Nickel and Dimed*, Picador (2011)

"[A]ccepting the persistence of widespread poverty even as the rich get ever richer is a choice that our politicians have made. And we should be ashamed of that choice."

  —PAUL KRUGMAN (economist), "Helping the Poor, the British Way,"
  The New York Times (December 25, 2006)

"You show me a capitalist, I'll show you a bloodsucker."

  —MALCOLM X, speech given in 1964

"What's been hardest is the way our legal system is structured to favor private property. I think people all over this city, of every background, would like to have the city government be able to determine which building goes where, how high it will be, who gets to live in it, what the rent will be. I think there's a socialistic impulse, which I hear every day, in every kind of community, that they would like things to be planned in accordance to their needs. And I would, too. Unfortunately, what stands in the way of that is hundreds of years of history that have elevated property rights and wealth to the point that that's the reality that calls the tune on a lot of development."

  —BILL DE BLASIO, Mayor of New York, *New York* magazine
  (September 4, 2017)

"Capitalism has not always existed in the world and will not always exist in the world."

   —ALEXANDRA OCASIO-CORTEZ, PBS interview, July 16, 2018.

Bernie Sanders, any speech.

CHAPTER 1

PEOPLE AND MARKETS

Human beings are not very good natural economists. People are not born with an intuitive understanding of the functioning of an economy. Our minds did not evolve to understand economics as studied by economists. Moreover, it is possible to be successful in a modern economy without understanding economics. It is also possible to live a rich and full life without ever learning economics. However, it is almost impossible to be a sensible voter. To understand why, it is necessary to digress and consider the environment in which our minds evolved.

Evolutionary Basis of Economic Understanding

Modern theories of the evolution of the mind indicate that our brains evolved to solve problems that persisted in the environment of evolutionary adaptation (EEA). This is the period when our ancestors were evolving to become human. It is generally thought that relatively little evolution has occurred since humans became civilized (in about the last ten thousand years), so much of our mental architecture is thought to have evolved in hunter-gatherer societies, and our minds are best adapted to such societies. (For a more detailed discussion of these issues, see Rubin 2002, Chapter 1.)

The human mind is not a "blank slate" (Pinker, 2003). Rather, the mind is preprogrammed for many activities and areas of understanding. The mind is organized into modules. Each module may be thought of as a special-purpose computer application, or "app," tasked with solving some problem. The preprogrammed problems are those that would have been relevant to surviving and reproducing in the evolutionary environment. For example, there is a module associated with language. There is a module for food and eating behavior. (This module, created in a world of scarce food, is not well adapted to modern living, where fat and sugar are all around us.) There are also modules associated with sex and mating behavior. All of these modules exist because it would simply be impossible for a general-purpose calculator to solve the problems that face a human being, and so the calculator (the brain) must be specialized to economize on reasoning power. Modules may be thought of like apps. It would be possible to program a computer to solve each problem that arises, but it would be too time-consuming, and such a computer would be almost useless. Rather, apps are created to solve problems that arise many times.

This notion was first associated with the study of learning of language. It would be impossible for an infant to learn language with no hardwired basis for such learning. It was the understanding of this difficulty that led psychologists to study the more general modularization of the mind. If there is a module for understanding economic behavior, then it should be associated with solving problems involving economic conditions in the EEA. In fact, there is no reason to expect that such a module exists.

There *is* a module associated with exchange and monitoring of human behavior. This is because trade arose early in our prehistory, and we developed a tool to monitor exchange and avoid being taken. In experiments involving logical relationships, subjects do better when they are told that the issues in the experiment have to do with monitoring of commitments and enforcing agreements than when the same problem is presented as a simple logical puzzle. This implies that we are adapted to avoid being cheated. However, it says nothing about any ability to observe efficiency or gains from trade (except those going to ourselves).

Anthropologists divide human existence into two basic periods. The key distinction is between mobile and sedentary societies, also called simple and complex or egalitarian and non-egalitarian hunter-gatherers, or foragers. By far the longest period of our existence as humans was the period spent as mobile hunter-gatherers. In this period, human groups were small, and there was little social structure, little food storage, and little division of labor or specialization. The only occupational specialization was by age.

Such people traveled light and did not have many possessions. The study of contemporary mobile hunter-gatherers is relevant because this lifestyle approximates the lifestyle in which we evolved, and so we are adapted to this mode of living. Thus, insights into the problems that arose in the period of nomadic hunter-gatherers would be relevant for understanding the hard-wired pattern of the mind.

When our ancestors settled down and began farming, there was great change. For example, occupational specialization became common. People began to possess physical goods, some of which were relatively large. Thus, this distinction occurred as our ancestors moved from a mobile to a sedentary lifestyle. By the time of large agricultural societies and the beginning of written history, specialization and division of labor were universal and important among humans. But this came late in our existence as humans—probably too late to have left a significant mark on our evolved preferences or intellects.

There was very little technological advance during the EEA. The pace of technological change in primitive societies seems amazingly slow by contemporary standards. For example, the Acheulean hand-axe tradition lasted for more than one million years in Africa, Asia, and Europe. In the Upper Paleolithic, about forty thousand years ago (when *Homo sapiens* had evolved), "major technological change" is defined as taking place when a change in stone techniques transpired over "a few thousand years." The Gravettian tradition in Europe lasted from about twenty-seven thousand to about twelve thousand years ago (all data from Gowlett, 1992). This sluggish rate of technological improvement may have been due to comparatively less-intelligent prehuman ancestors in the early periods. It can be understood as being due to low levels of population and hence fewer individuals to create new technologies and perhaps poorly defined property rights in innovations (Jones, 2001). Given this low rate of technological change and innovation, there was no incentive to evolve a mental mechanism for understanding or rewarding innovation.

There was little growth—so little that no individual would observe any growth over his or her lifetime (Kremer, 1993). Each person would live and die in a world of constant technology and income. Thus, there was no incentive to evolve a mechanism for understanding or planning for growth. Indeed, to the extent that our ancestors may have had a subsistence level of income, any changes in circumstances were more likely to be harmful than beneficial, so they would have tended to be leery of change.

There were, however, possibilities for exchange, and so a monitoring mechanism to limit shirking was useful. Some exchange would be of simple goods: one forager may have more nuts, another more berries, and exchange would occur. A common and important form of exchange would have been exchange over time of the same good. If I have a successful hunt this week, I may give you some of the meat in expectation that you will reciprocate next week. For individuals living on the margin of subsistence, such exchange of the same good at different times could have been extremely important for survival.

Shirking or social cheating could have been in the form of refusal to provide one's share if successful (the EEA form of tax evasion) or not spending sufficient effort on hunting, planning instead to benefit from others' work (the EEA form of welfare fraud). In such a world, if someone had substantially more than others, it may have been the result of unwillingness to share or reciprocate for past benefits received. Foragers pay careful attention to this behavior and punish those who are perceived as not sharing sufficiently. It would have been important for individuals to monitor the terms of such exchange to avoid being victimized or cheated. Thus, if someone accumulated a significant amount of wealth, it was probably the result of shirking of one sort or another.

This is a world of strong reciprocity and of a form of exchange that anthropologists call equality matching, which Pinker (2003) claims is the core of intuitive economics. It is contrasted with market pricing, the system economists study. When there is a mismatch between the two systems, then hostility and conflict can result. An example is found in Waldfogel (1993), who used market pricing methods to analyze Christmas giving, a transaction normally analyzed using equality matching. To an economist, all giving should be in the form of cash, because this will maximize its value to the recipient. If I give you a shirt that you would have bought anyway, then you are just as well off as if I had given you cash. If I give you anything that you would not have bought, you are worse off than if I gave you cash. However, people have not ceased buying Christmas or Hanukkah presents and replaced them with cash. (When I suggested this to my wife, who is a pretty good intuitive economist, she did not bother to answer.)

Shirking could also have occurred through not providing one's share in cooperative ventures. Cooperation was useful in hunting big game and in primitive warfare. Both activities were dangerous, and so there would have been strong incentives for shirking to avoid being killed or injured. Modern foragers spend much time analyzing the social behavior of associates to monitor shirking. The monitoring module could have evolved to monitor these activities in an economy with little specialization and little division of labor.

To summarize: We evolved in situations of little specialization and division of labor, little capital, low technological change, and little or no economic growth. There was some exchange, including exchange of the same good over time, and possibilities of shirking. If there were significant wealth inequalities, they were probably due to shirking by refusing to share. If our minds evolved in this situation, then current innate economic modules should be adapted to this setting, and this appears to be the case. In particular, what was lacking were any modules for understanding the social benefits of exchange, economic growth, investment, or innovation.

This is not to say that people cannot understand economics. Our minds are sufficiently flexible and sufficiently powerful to learn and understand many things that were not part of the EEA. A useful analogy is reading and speech. All humans growing up in a normal environment learn speech without any conscious effort; the basic pattern of speech is hard-wired. But reading must be taught. Our minds are not hard-wired to be able to read. Economics is like reading: it can be learned, but it must be taught. Moreover, some aspects of economics are very difficult to understand (Leiser and Shemesh, 2018).

Economics and Politics

The analysis in this section is based on my work on the biology of politics (Rubin, 2002, 2003, 2014a, 2014b). We are a hierarchical species, and so politics has always been important. Based on that work, I have concluded that political thinking is more basic to our minds than economic thinking. That is, when faced with an interpersonal issue that does not involve family or sex, an individual untrained in economics is more likely to treat it as a political issue than an economic issue. Political thinking was important for our ancestors; economic thinking was not. Thus, the political module is innate and more basic than the economic way of thinking, which must be learned. Indeed, one of our tasks as economists is, or should be, to educate our students and the public that there is this distinction. Pinker (2003), not an economist, argues that economics is one area where human intuitions are lacking, and that it is important to teach economics for this reason, and Leiser and Shemesh (2018) make the same point. If we treat an economic problem as if it were a political problem, we are likely to get the wrong answer.

Here are some of the relevant characteristics of political thinking as contrasted with economic thinking:

1. Politics is about competition for resources, while economics is about cooperation to generate surpluses.
2. Political thinking tends to be zero-sum—division of a fixed pie. Economics allows for positive-sum interactions.
3. Politics is an "us versus them" conflict. We are a tribal species, with tribal competition. Economics is universal; trade with anyone is beneficial.
4. Perhaps because of its "us versus them" nature, politics is dichotomous: win or lose, good or bad. Economics is continuous: more or less, how much.
5. Political processes are controlled by specific active agents: the chief, the king, the general. These agents may be heroes or villains, but they are purposeful agents. Economics deals with processes, such as the market process or the "invisible hand."
6. Politics focuses on motives; economics focuses on net outputs.

I now briefly discuss each of these issues in turn. Each is considered in more detail in the following chapters.

Competition

The most important error in economic thinking is associated with one of the most fundamental concepts of economics: competition. As

Nobel laureate James Buchanan (1964) has argued, the fundamental unit of economics is the transaction, and transactions are cooperative. Competition is important, but it is a tool to improve cooperation. Buchanan, among others, points out that in the purely competitive model, there is no competition, but we economists do not fully understand or analyze the implications. Even in non-perfectly competitive environments, the degree of "competition" is overestimated. Firms in this environment do compete with one another, but they are competing for the right to cooperate with consumers and suppliers, including workers. A monopolist is a firm with an exclusive ability or right to cooperate with consumers in some market.

One reason we humans focus on competition rather than cooperation is due to our political bias toward looking at markets through the lens of politics. Competition is between firms, who are actively striving to accomplish some goal. We naturally look at these firms as actors. But the cooperative market is a process, with no particular actors. Even the "invisible hand" metaphor is in a deep sense a political metaphor—it implies that there is some actor or agent directing the process. Of course, Adam Smith knew that this was a metaphor, but he also understood that the human mind could best understand the process if it were presented as the result of the actions of a conscious agent: one with a "hand," albeit invisible.

If economists had defined the fundamental economic model in terms of cooperation rather than competition, our entire understanding of economics by untrained persons might have changed. Humans often tend to view competition as bad and cooperation as good. Because our terminology leads us to think of competition rather than cooperation in markets, even believers in a market often feel that they must justify markets (Brooks 2010). That is, competition is viewed as a "cost" and defenders of markets believe that there must be some offsetting benefit to justify this cost. If we used the language of cooperation, then many who are critical of capitalism might have different attitudes.

Both "competition" and "cooperation" are metaphors. What is really going on in a market (or in any area of human behavior) is an attempt by human actors to maximize their utility—to do the best they can. The outside observers come along and characterize the behavior: "That is cooperative" or "That is competitive." But it is the actual behavior that is important, and our characterization less so.

Zero-Sum Thinking

Political thinking is zero-sum or even negative-sum, as when there is a resource-using conflict over a resource. This may be because the economy during evolutionary times was not dynamic or growing, and so there was no need for our minds to evolve to understand economic growth. We naturally think of a fixed amount of goods to divide. In such a world, if I have more, then you have less—zero-sum. If we fight over the resource, then we have less in total because of the loss from the act of fighting—negative-sum. This sort of thinking permeates the decision-making of those untrained in economics. For example, it explains why untrained people worry about losing jobs through international trade. (The number of jobs is viewed as fixed.)

Economists understand economic growth. But although we understand positive-sum interactions, we are also sometimes subject to zero-sum thinking. Recently the profession has begun to worry about increasing income inequality (Piketty and Saez, 2003). But inequality is only an issue in a zero-sum world. If we economists believe our own theories of earnings and productivity, then one person earns more money than another because the higher earner is more productive, and earnings are directly related to productivity—to "marginal revenue product" in the jargon of economics. In a zero-sum world, inequality is an issue because if one person has more, then another has less. But in a world of modern economics, inequality is not or should not be an issue.

If one person has more than another, it is because the richer person is more productive. If the richer person earns less, this will not provide any benefit to the poorer person; it will simply reduce total wealth.

Us Versus Them

Evolutionary human competition is within an "us versus them" structure. The evolutionary period was a period of much conflict, and often tribes would compete with others, often through small-scale wars (Pinker, 2011). It was important to look for signs of aggression from neighbors. It was also sometimes important to be the aggressor.

Our minds naturally seek this structure. Thus, when the economy is defined in terms of competition, we look for competitors and rivals. These competitors may be other firms, even though in many forms of competition there is no rival. They may also be thought of in terms of firms and customers. For example, the entire "consumerist" movement associated with Ralph Nader and his associates thinks of the economy as being one in which firms and customers are fundamentally enemies. Firms are viewed as predators, and consumers as prey. In fact, of course, firms and customers are in a cooperative arrangement, with only minor details (the division of the surpluses through price) being the subject of disagreement. This form of thinking also leads us to seek villains, as discussed below.

This is especially important when considering international trade. Here, the combination of zero-sum thinking and us-versus-them thinking leads to a particularly toxic mix. We tend to think that Americans are losing jobs (because of zero-sum thinking: the number of jobs is viewed as fixed), and we are losing them to foreigners—to members of another tribe. This leads to anti-trade policies, such as tariffs and quotas. Of course, American firms that produce the same goods that are being imported and workers through unions that domestically produce these goods are perfectly happy to exploit this sort of zero-sum, us-versus-them thinking, but the thinking exists independently of the exploitation. This sort of thinking explains in part why protectionists have been more successful than many other interest groups at convincing the public to provide benefits to the interest group at the expense of the public, in the form of higher-priced goods. It also explains why we sometimes refer to "trade wars."

Us-versus-them thinking also underlines the costliest error in human history: Marxism. There are many fallacies in Marxist analysis, mostly due to primitive economic thinking, as discussed later. In this context, however, what is relevant is the Marxist view of class competition, particularly labor versus capital. In Marx's view, labor and capital are in competition. In reality, both are needed for production, and they work together cooperatively to produce output. More recent theories of "race, class, and gender" commit the same fallacy: They view the world in us-versus-them terms, rather than in cooperative terms.

Agents Versus Processes

In politics, outcomes are driven by the actions of specific agents: the chief, king, general, parliament, minister. Moreover, these agents are identifiable: We know who they are. Economic activities are much more process-driven. There are active agents in economics—entrepreneurs—but economic theory does not actually handle these agents very well. Kahneman (2011) makes the point that in general our minds think of agents rather than processes.

When things go well, we look for someone to praise, rather than understanding that it is often the result of a well-functioning market process. Conversely, when a process goes awry, we do not view it as a systemic failure. Rather, we seek to blame someone. This is the converse of our lack of understanding of the invisible hand. Just as we do not understand intuitively that unplanned and uncontrolled processes can generate beneficial equilibria, so we do not understand that such processes can go awry and sometimes generate harmful equilibria with no one being to blame. Economists are also subject to this particular fallacy. Because we believe in invisible-hand processes leading to desirable outcomes, we are perhaps unwilling to accept that these processes can on occasion fail with no one to blame. (An exception is Thomas Schelling, 1978.)

Ex post—after the fact—we can always find some way in which a harmful outcome could have been prevented by some active agent, but that does not mean that ex ante—before the fact—it was caused by some failure of that agent to take action. Ex ante there may be many possible failures, and it may be impossible to determine which will occur. It may also be that if we take an action to prevent one failure, it will cause another, so that in some circumstances some systemic failure is inevitable. For example, if we are in a "bubble," then if the monetary authorities stop the bubble, there may well be an immediate crash. Allowing it to continue will ultimately lead to a perhaps even worse crash. But if the authorities stop the bubble now, they will be blamed for the immediate crash. If they don't, they will eventually be blamed for the ultimate crash.

Belief in the importance of conscious agents rather than impersonal processes often leads people to blame others for unfortunate events. For example, when the price of some commodity increases, many will hold "greedy" companies to blame, although those trained in economics may understand that it a result of the normal functioning of the market. When there is an increase in oil prices, it is common for the political authorities, in response to popular unhappiness, to assign the Federal Trade Commission (FTC) the task of "investigating" the source of this increase. A year or two later, when popular anger has dissipated, the FTC reports that the price increase was the result of market forces. But if people understood the impersonality of the market, there would be no need for the investigation.

Belief in the power of conscious agents also leads to a belief in conspiracy theories. Nozick (1977) and Sunstein and Vermeule (2009) discuss the difference between conspiracy theories, theories that argue that processes which seem random are actually due to conscious actions, and "hidden hand" or "invisible hand" theories, which argue the opposite: organized processes which seem directed by a conscious agent are actually the result of blind processes. Economics is, of course, the mother of invisible-hand theories. The Darwinian theory of evolution is another example of a successful invisible-hand theory, as is the evolution of language.

Pipes (1999) has shown the harm caused by conspiracy theories. A particularly pernicious conspiracy theory is embodied in a volume called *The Protocols of the Elders of Zion*. This is a text fabricated by agents of the Russian Czar and first published in 1903. It purports to show a group of elderly Jews conspiring to control the world. It "explains" many events as being the result of this conspiracy. Henry Ford believed this fraud and publicized it, and it greatly influenced Adolf Hitler. Even now, many believe that Jews are extremely powerful because of remnants of conspiracy thinking. Such thinking is common among neo-Nazis and among many Muslims, and the *Protocols* have been endorsed by several leaders of Muslim states. It is one of the bases of modern anti-Semitism. A major theme is that Jews control the economy. Some have even claimed that Jews control the weather.

A belief in conspiracy theories of the economy is inconsistent with a belief in the actual way markets function. It is, however, consistent with a fear and dislike of markets. If the results of a market process are due to a hidden conspiracy, then there is no reason to allow markets to continue to function. A little search on the internet can show that some still believe in conspiracy theories.

On the other side, if we see the outcome of a market process, we can then say that we did not need the market to generate that outcome, and that a government agency could have achieved the same outcome by direct control. But that does not mean that ex ante the agency would have known what to do. As Buchanan (1964) discusses, the outcome is the result of a market process, and as Hayek (1945) points out, the information needed to accomplish the goal has been generated by the market itself. Many things that seem obvious ex post are by no means so obvious ex ante. Moreover, this fallacy leads to a belief in "industrial policy" and other efforts at government planning, such as picking winners and losers. Since ex post we believe that government could have achieved the same favorable outcome as the market actually achieved, we then believe that ex ante government could plan for good outcomes.

Motives Versus Outputs

In politics, motives matter. Is the chief trying to improve the welfare of the people, or is he trying to maximize the welfare of himself and his close associates? The answer to this question is important because the outcome of the political process is direct. An evil king will produce evil results. This is perhaps a corollary of the zero-sum nature of politics and of evolutionary societies: If the king takes more, there is less for the rest of us. This applies to goods and services, and to sexual and therefore reproductive success (Betzig, 1986). Even today, the honesty or lack thereof of a political candidate is an important part of many political campaigns.

One of Adam Smith's great insights is that in economics, outputs matter; motives do not. In the market, selfish and greedy people can produce socially desirable results. This insight is one of the most difficult for noneconomists to grasp. For example, I write a lot about the pharmaceutical industry. The most common criticism of this industry is that "they are out for profits, not to help the sick." Anyone conversant with economics would say, "Of course. So what? The way to make profits is to help the sick." But physicians and others writing about the industry reject or ignore this argument. They focus on inputs (motives) and not on outputs (beneficial drugs).

Even some defenders of capitalism sometimes commit this error. Markets reward people for their output—for what they produce.

Defenders often argue that wealthy people are deserving of their money because they are talented, or because they work hard, or because they save and invest. All of these may be true, but they are irrelevant. Markets reward people if they produce things that other people value and are willing to pay for. Rewards may be due to hard work, but equally they may be due to luck or even to seemingly immoral behavior, sometimes called "sharp practices." It does not matter. It is only what is produced that is relevant.

It is also argued that it is good for the wealthy to "give back"—that is, to donate some of their wealth to charitable causes. This may be socially beneficial if the charitable causes are themselves socially beneficial—although for many wealthy persons who feel guilty about their wealth, the charities themselves may be harmful and opposed to markets (Schumpeter, 1942). The notion of giving back assumes that the person has taken from others in order to make his or her money. But this is not true: the creation of wealth is a socially benign and useful process. The good done by the person in earning that wealth is much greater than any benefit from the charitable contributions, and there is no need to apologize for earning a lot of money. By making automobiles cheap and readily available to millions of people, Henry Ford (not himself a good person; he was a vicious anti-Semite) did vastly more good (for everyone, including Jews) than has the Ford Foundation. By making computers ubiquitous, Bill Gates did more good than the Gates Foundation is likely to do.

In producing wealth it is necessary to benefit people by satisfying their desires, but in giving back it is possible to do harm as well as good, depending on the targets of giving. For example, the Koch brothers and George Soros both give back by contributing large sums to political action, but it is impossible that they are both contributing to social good since the causes they advocate are diametrically opposed. (My views on who creates social benefits should be obvious.)

In the next chapter, I discuss zero-sum thinking in more detail.

CHAPTER 2

REALLY BASIC ECONOMICS: ZERO-SUM THINKING AND COMPETITION

In this chapter, I discuss the nature and importance of what is called "zero-sum" thinking, and I show how this sort of thinking is related to the use of the term "competition."

The terms "zero-sum," "positive-sum," and "negative-sum" are originally from a branch of economics and mathematics called game theory. A zero-sum game is one where the winnings and losses add up to zero. That is, whatever the winners gain is equal to whatever the losers lose. An example is a group of friends playing poker. At the end of an evening of poker, if we ask the winners how much they won and ask the losers how much they lost (and if everyone tells the truth), then the sum must be zero—a zero-sum game. Games and sports are often zero-sum. Some are even negative-sum: The losers lose more than the winners gain. An example would be a poker game at a casino, where the "house" takes part of each pot. Here, winnings of the winners are less than losses to the losers, with the house taking the difference. In positive-sum situations, there are net gains. Winners gain more than losers lose.

The economy is positive-sum. In general, most economic interactions are positive-sum. That is, in most situations the sum of gains and losses is positive: the gainers gain more than the losers lose. A moment's thought should indicate that this is true, since we are now much richer than our ancestors. This would not be true unless positive-sum interactions were possible. If almost all of us are richer than our parents and grandparents, and all of us are richer than our great-grandparents, it must be because the world is richer, and the world can only be richer if positive-sum interactions are possible. Indeed, all voluntary transactions, which are the heart of economics, are positive-sum.

There are also negative-sum interactions in economics, generally associated with involuntary transactions. Sometimes the gains to winners are less than losses to losers. For example, a thief steals a piece of jewelry worth $50,000 and sells it to a fence for $10,000. The fence then melts it down and sells the components—the gold, the stones— for $15,000. This is a negative-sum interaction: The loss to the owner of the jewelry is greater than the gain to the thief. A piece of jewelry worth $50,000 has been melted down and turned into ingredients worth $15,000, so there is a real loss of $35,000. Another common negative-sum interaction is a lawsuit. A sues B for $100,000; A and B each pay their lawyers $30,000. A wins; B pays him $100,000. But B has paid $130,000 in total (a $100,000 verdict plus $30,000 in legal fees) and A only nets $70,000 ($100,000 minus $30,000 in legal fees), so the net is negative-sum between A and B. As we will see, government regulations can also mandate negative-sum interactions. However, all of these situations represent nonvoluntary, coerced transactions.

The Pie Metaphor of Economics

Any economic interaction has two components. These are often described as the "size of the pie" and the "division of the pie." The size of the pie is the positive- or negative-sum aspect of the interaction: Does the interaction lead to larger or smaller wealth in total? The division of the pie is the part of the interaction that determines who gets what is left, the zero-sum aspect of the interaction.

However, the two aspects are not independent of each other. Rules establishing the division of the pie create incentives, and these incentives then affect the size of the pie. We can change the rule for division or we can change the rule for creation, but we cannot change both simultaneously. For example, if we have a rule that says, "Everyone gets equal shares," then people will not work as hard and pies will be smaller. If we have a rule that says, "Shares are proportional to inputs," then pies will be larger, but division will be unequal. Any scheme for distribution of the pie is somewhere between these extremes. Society must decide on the terms of the trade-off between "equity" (the division of the pie, what is sometimes called fairness) and efficiency (the size of the pie). The question about equity is not whether distribution is fair or not; there is some trade-off, and we must decide as a society how much income we are willing to give up for more equity. "Fairness" is not free.

The notion of a trade-off between two desirable outcomes (wealth and fairness) is not intuitive; humans tend to believe that "good begets good," so that good processes (that is, efficient ones) are associated with good outcomes (fairness and equality) (Leiser and Shemesh, 2018). Actually, the world is made up of trade-offs. Politicians often talk as if there are no trade-offs and their favored policies will generate only good things, but actually there are always costs. For example, "If we develop green nonpolluting energy sources, then incomes will become more evenly distributed." When in fact nonpolluting energy will lead to increased income inequality because the poor spend a larger portion of their incomes on energy than do the rich.

The thesis of this chapter is simple: As human beings, our natural way of interpreting events is zero-sum. That is, in many situations we focus on division of the pie, on who gets more and who gets less. But most real interactions (as opposed to artificial interactions, like a poker game or an athletic contest) have effects on the total amount of wealth—on the size of the pie. Looking at positive-sum or negative-sum interactions as if they were zero-sum can lead to confusion. Moreover, in making economic policy, focusing on the zero-sum aspect of policy can lead to bad decisions. Finally, an emphasis on "competition" in discussing an economy tends to reinforce these tendencies toward zero-sum thinking.

Economists are trained to look at the effects on the total amount of wealth. Indeed, looking at these effects is the heart and soul of economics. This is what economists mean by "efficiency" or "inefficiency." Efficient interactions are positive-sum; inefficient ones are negative-sum. It is not difficult to examine these effects, but it does not come naturally to humans. Some training is needed. Economists as teachers should provide this training.

But we don't always do so. This is because the nonzero-sum nature of economic thinking is so ingrained and so natural a part of our worldview as economists that we don't always bother to explain it. We are "mind-blind" to the nonzero-sum nature of transactions, or we suffer from what is called the "curse of knowledge." That is, the notion that there are positive-sum interactions is so ingrained among economists that we often do not even think to mention it. The "curse of knowledge" says that sometimes people assume too much knowledge on the part of listeners or readers, so that our explanations go beyond them. Pinker (2014) claims that this error is the most important explanation for unintelligible writing. I believe that economists suffer from this curse with respect to zero-sum and nonzero-sum interactions.

The result is often that our policy proposals as economists go right by the citizens we are trying to talk to. Even in teaching students, we often start at too high a level. We assume that students understand that some interactions can lead to an increased or reduced size of the pie, and we don't always bother to explain this point. We talk about efficient and inefficient interactions, but the basic idea may get lost in the graphs and the jargon. We do explain gains from trade when we talk about international trade, but we should do it much sooner in the principles of economics course. Gains from trade exist in all voluntary transactions, but we may only mention them in one context. All exchanges lead to gains from trade, but we often do not discuss them. Explaining in more detail the nature of gains from trade is one way in which economists can increase our social value.

This chapter is not about "basic" economics, as generally understood. This chapter is about pre-basic economics, or "really basic economics." Basic economics focuses on analyzing interactions (usually in markets) and showing the effects of these interactions on efficiency and on the size of the pie. This chapter deals with issues that come before basic economics. Rather than showing which sorts of interactions are efficient, this chapter is aimed at showing that size-of-the-pie effects (efficiency effects) are important and that questions about the size-of-the-pie effects should be asked. After people learn to ask if there are such effects, we can then go on to the basic economic questions of what the effects are and how to design policies to achieve the effects we want. But until people learn that there are effects on the size of the pie from all economic policies, they won't know to look for these effects. And if people are thinking about the distribution-of-the-pie effects while economists are talking about size of the pie, there will be no communication. As an economist recently said to me in a discussion of zero-sum thinking, "Now I understand why my sister never knows what I am talking about."

This chapter is aimed at those who don't know what we economists are talking about. Granted, sometimes we economists talk in esoteric terms and use language or mathematics that is difficult to understand. This is especially true when we are talking to one another, although, as discussed below, it too often pervades our discussions with undergraduates. But sometimes we try to communicate using ordinary English. Even when we do, we are often difficult to understand. We may be talking to citizens and writing op-eds to explain policies. We may be testifying before legislative committees or in court. We may be talking to our students or writing textbooks for them. But in many cases our listeners don't know what we are talking about because we are talking about positive- or negative-sum policies, and our listeners are thinking about a zero-sum world. If people don't know what we are talking about, this is because we have not explained ourselves enough. We may be presenting the results of basic economics, but we need to start with really basic economics. Really basic economics is not hard, so if you don't know what an economist is talking about, it is because he or she has not explained him- or herself well enough. This chapter aims at providing that explanation.

As I explain some of the implications of zero-sum thinking, it will appear that there are inconsistencies. This is correct. Zero-sum thinking is erroneous, and so the implications of this form of thinking will also be erroneous, and inconsistent. (It is a principle of logic that from false premises, anything can be proven, including inconsistent results.) Most people do not think long and hard about economic principles, and so it is possible for them to believe inconsistent things. If confronted, they may realize that something they believe must be wrong, but mostly people are not confronted with the implications of their ideas, and so nothing stops them from believing inconsistent things. For example, many people believe that taxes are too high and that government should do more things, and do them better. These positions are inconsistent—to do more requires more resources which must come from taxes. Similarly, people may complain about high prices and poor service in a restaurant, without considering that better service requires higher prices. Thus, an economist reading this book may say, "People cannot believe both of those statements. Rubin must be wrong." But they can believe both if they never consider them at the same time, or if they never consider the interrelationship between them.

Zero-sum thinking violates the laws of economics. It assumes that we can set price and quantity independently of each other, or that we can affect the rules of distribution without affecting the amount to be distributed. In that sense, zero-sum thinking is a form of magic. Normal magic violates the rules of physics or biology (spinning gold from flax, growing beanstalks to additional worlds). Zero-sum thinking is a form of magical thinking in that it violates the rules of economics. The great economist Milton Friedman understood the magical nature of erroneous economic thinking when he asked if we expected the "tooth fairy" to pay for excess spending. That is, when people asked the government to provide more goods and services but not increase taxes, Friedman asked how the benefits would be paid for; would the "tooth fairy" (a magical creature) provide the money?

In this chapter, I analyze several areas of economic policy: wages, welfare policy, taxes, law, international trade, and globalization. In each case I consider first zero-sum thinking about the issue. I then show why this sort of thinking is incorrect and discuss positive-sum (efficiency) issues related to the issue. I also consider some noneconomic aspects of zero-sum thinking. Finally, I digress to discuss the role of mathematics in teaching economics. I begin with a discussion of zero-sum thinking.

A misunderstanding of economics is not unique. There are many areas where our "intuitive" or "folk" beliefs are inconsistent with scientific understanding. Shtulman (2017) describes in detail many scientific areas where people's intuition is incorrect. The three characteristics of intuitive theories are the following: First, intuitive theories are coherent in that they embody a consistent set of beliefs. Second, intuitive theories are widespread; many people have the same set of beliefs. Third, the theories are robust in that they are beliefs held by many people in many places and times. They are commonly the set of beliefs we develop as children and use to understand the world.

Zero-sum thinking is exactly consistent with these characteristics. There is a set of beliefs that forms a mostly coherent view of the world, although if pushed there are inconsistencies in this set of beliefs. They are widespread; most untrained individuals have zero-sum beliefs. It is also difficult to root out these beliefs, and even strong evidence does not convince many of their falsity. They are also consistent with the economic world of children, in that most interactions between children are in fact zero-sum.

What Is Zero-Sum Thinking?

Zero-sum thinking is thinking that something is fixed. Of course, some things are fixed in value, but in many cases people think that things are fixed when in fact they are variable. As I will show, economics teaches that many things are variable which appear at first glance to be fixed. Indeed, I believe that erroneous zero-sum thinking is the major source of errors in economic policy. Zero-sum thinking leads us to stress the fixed sum, "division-of-the-pie" aspect of a problem, rather than the "size-of-the-pie" issues, which are much more important. You can only divide the pie you have, so its size is crucial.

Part of the reason for zero-sum thinking is ignoring second- and third-order effects. When something changes, this change will lead to reactions and additional changes in response. Economics studies these reactions and responses. However, zero-sum thinking ignores them and assumes that one change is the end of the sequence. For example, the first-order effect of an increase in minimum wages is that some workers will earn more. The second-order effect, however, is that fewer workers will be employed. The third-order effect is that some people will not be trained in basic work skills such as punctuality because they are not hired. But a well-meaning person looking only at the first-order effect will advocate laws that actually harm the people he or she is trying to benefit.

There are two alternatives to a zero-sum interaction: the world may be positive-sum (one in which gains are greater than losses) or negative-sum (one in which losses are greater than gains). Voluntary transactions are positive-sum: both parties gain from these transactions, as described in the chapter on cooperation. Fights or conflicts, including litigation, are generally negative-sum: resources are expended in the contest, so that the amount won by the winners is less than the amount lost by the losers, and jointly the parties lose. Of course, the parties are aware of these potential losses, which is why rational people try to avoid conflict. Most disputes do not become lawsuits, and most lawsuits settle out of court. Most labor contracts are negotiated without a strike. Few border conflicts lead to war. Few arguments lead to physical violence.

As an example of zero-sum thinking, consider the concept of "needs." Noneconomists often talk about needs. "People need a certain amount of food." "People need a place to live." "People need access to health care." This implies that the amount of food or shelter or medical care is fixed and immutable. The concept of need implies that people purchase a certain constant amount of each good because that is what they "need." In fact, there is no objective measure of needs in an advanced economy. We may need a certain number of calories to survive, but almost no one in a country like America is in any real danger of starvation. Beyond this, everything we consume is a result of preferences and prices. For example, it might appear that we "need" somewhere to live. But when the economy turns down, it becomes obvious that many young people can remain at home with their parents; what they needed when they could find high-paying jobs is not the same as what is needed when working at McDonald's. Or someone living in Cincinnati may "need" a two thousand-square-foot apartment, but in New York, where rents are vastly higher, he or she may only "need" one thousand square feet shared with one or two roommates.

The most fundamental principle of economics is the "law of demand." This law says that people purchase more of a good (any good) as the price falls, and less as the price rises. The law of demand is exactly the opposite of the concept of need. If we really needed something, then our consumption would not respond to price changes. But the law of demand says that the amount of something we consume does in fact respond to changes in price. Moreover, demand shifts more as consumers have longer times to adjust. Thus, even if needs drive our demand in the short run, in the longer run we can adapt more and the amount we purchase can change greatly.

The concept of need is an example of zero-sum thinking, and the law of demand shows that it is erroneous. When price increases, the first-order effect may be to purchase the same quantity (the amount we "need") and spend more on that good. But second- and third-order effects allow for changes in consumption. For example, if the price of gasoline increases, the immediate effect may be to drive the same amount as before and spend more on gasoline. But second-order effects allow for rearranging our lives to conserve on gasoline—perhaps by carpooling. Third-order effects might include buying a more efficient car or even moving closer to our job. The concept of "need" would ignore all of these effects.

Our minds tend to view the world through a zero-sum lens. That is, our natural way of thinking about issues is zero-sum. This may be because we evolved in a zero-sum world, or it may be because in the short run many things seem to be fixed, and so zero-sum thinking works for many issues. But even though our natural way of thinking is zero-sum, we can be taught to think in positive-sum terms. Indeed, teaching that the world is not zero-sum is one of the most important functions of teaching economics.

There are many sources of zero-sum thinking. In many respects, the world appears to be zero-sum. When we are young, if Johnny gets more candy, Suzie gets less. Even as we grow older, many aspects of the world seem to be fixed: there are only so many rutabagas in Kroger's on a given day, and if I buy them all you can't get any. If I get a job at Emory, someone else does not get that job. If Suzie gets into Harvard, Johnny does not. Zero-sum thinking is like flat-earth thinking: for many issues, assuming the earth is flat will work, and so will zero-sum thinking. I can get where I am going using a flat two-dimensional map. Indeed, with a GPS I don't even need to consider the shape of my route. It is only if we are cartographers or astronomers or pilots on international routes that we need consider the curvature of the earth. Similarly, for many day-to-day decisions, zero-sum thinking will work. It is only if we are economists studying the economy or if we are policymakers trying to achieve economic growth or other policy goals that we need understand that the world is not zero-sum.

But it is exactly because policymakers must consider nonzero-sum aspects of the world that it is important for all of us to understand that the world is not zero-sum. In a democracy, voters elect politicians who ultimately decide policy. If voters have in their heads a fallacious or magical model of the world, they will elect politicians who either believe in this model themselves or pretend to, and who in either case adopt policies based on the fallacious model. In this sense, it is more important for citizens to understand fundamental economics than it is to understand that the world is round. For most people, there is no cost to thinking that the world is flat, but there is a real cost if voters think that the world is zero-sum.

An Example: The 2016 U.S. Election

Donald Trump and Bernie Sanders might seem unlikely economic soulmates, but they shared a mistaken reliance on zero-sum thinking and long discredited economic policies during the 2016 election.

48

Mr. Trump's anti-immigration and anti-trade positions make him essentially a disciple of mercantilism, a protectionist economic theory refuted by Adam Smith in 1776. Bernie Sanders proudly calls himself a socialist and advocates vast increases in taxes and government power. The history of the past century, from the Soviet Union's fall to the collapse of Venezuela, amply shows that a socialist economy isn't only "rigged," to borrow one of Mr. Sanders's favorite words—it doesn't work.

Messrs. Trump and Sanders have been led astray by zero-sum thinking or the assumption that economic magnitudes are fixed when they are in fact variable.

If the world is zero-sum, then the number of jobs is fixed, as is gross domestic product. In Mr. Trump's mind, if there are more Mexican workers in the U.S., then American workers must lose their jobs. In the real, positive-sum world where Mr. Trump doesn't live, Mexican workers also consume, thus increasing GDP and creating new jobs.

Moreover, the reason that firms hire immigrant workers is to lower costs, and this leads to lower prices for consumers, allowing them to purchase additional goods and adding new jobs to the U.S. economy. But in a fixed world, prices do not change, so this effect is ignored.

Similar arguments apply to Mr. Trump's analysis of Chinese imports. In a world of fixed GDP and prices, imports of goods from China merely replace goods that otherwise would have been produced by American workers. In the real world, imports reduce prices and increase GDP, so workers, who are also consumers, benefit from imports of lower-cost goods and increase their consumption of other goods.

Mr. Sanders's economics is also zero-sum, although he emphasizes a different aspect of the fallacy. In a zero-sum world, taxes don't matter much because people work the same amount anyway, so there are no losses from reduced effort in response to higher taxes. Similarly, in a zero-sum world, methods of production are given, so there are no responses to changing prices: higher minimum wages don't lead to layoffs, for example. (In the real world, we saw Walmart's recent store closings following wage increases, and reductions in number of servers in restaurants in response to increased minimum wages for tipped workers.) In the Bernie Sanders universe, the size of the economy is fixed so there is plenty to redistribute no matter how misguided the economic policies.

Zero-sum thinking persists because it is superficially appealing. Mr. Trump's policies would in theory benefit Americans and increase jobs. Mr. Sanders's policies would make the poor better off. In the actual, positive-sum world we live in, their policies—building a fence along the Mexican border, disrupting labor markets by deporting millions of productive workers, huge tariffs on imported goods, much higher income taxes and minimum wages—would, if adopted, lead to an economic depression that would make the 1930s look prosperous.

Zero-Sum Thinking and Competition

What does the use of the term "competition" as used by economists have to do with zero-sum thinking? The competition metaphor in economics was borrowed from sports. Sport is, of course, the essence of a zero-sum activity: there are winners and losers, and the position of every contestant is relative to the other contestants. My absolute speed in a race does not matter; all that matters is my speed relative to the other runners.

When noneconomists think of competition, the mental notion is also of a zero-sum activity. The term competition applied to the economy reinforces our bias toward zero-sum thinking. Two workers want the same job; they compete for the job. One outcompetes the other and gets the job, an apparent zero-sum outcome. A similar situation occurs when two businesses are in the same market, or when two consumers want the same product. Focusing on the competition involved forces our mind into the zero-sum paradigm of winners and losers, as in sports, because it focuses our minds on the competitors themselves and on the zero-sum nature of the interaction. Moreover, there is a tendency to feel sympathy for the losers. Behavioral economists have shown that people feel losses more deeply than equal-sized gains. That is, the sadness of losing $1,000 is greater than the happiness of gaining $1,000. When we read about or observe someone losing in a competition, we feel more sympathy for the loser than we feel joy for the winner, so what appears to be a zero-sum outcome may be viewed as a negative-sum event (unless it is our team winning.)

But look at the issue through another lens: the lens of cooperation. For what are the two workers competing? They are competing to be hired by the company—they are competing for the right to cooperate with the employer. The worker who is hired is hired because the manager believes that he or she will produce more for the firm than the non-hired worker. That is a positive-sum outcome. That is, employers hire the worker who will provide the greatest output for the firm. Similarly, when one firm has more customers than another, this is because the more successful firm does a better job of cooperating by offering consumers what they want, a positive-sum outcome. That is, it is exactly that the successful firm does a better job cooperating with its customers. If Walmart has more business than Mom & Pop's Haberdashery, it is exactly because Walmart provides more valuable services to customers than does M&P. M&P loses when Walmart takes its business, but consumers gain, and the gains to Walmart plus the gains to consumers are greater than the losses to M&P. That is, if consumers switch from M&P to Walmart, the result is positive-sum, not zero-sum. It is because we focus on the competition between Walmart and M&P and ignore the benefits to the consumer that we think of the transaction as competitive and zero-sum and may feel sorry for M&P or pass a law banning Walmart.

Moreover, as mentioned above, we may put more weight on the losses suffered by M&P than on the gains to Walmart. This is partially because we generally value losses more than gains, but also because we may feel sympathy for the underdog and may more easily identify with M&P (we may even know Mom or Pop or their kids) than with a big corporation in Arkansas or its stockholders. Because Walmart is the big guy and M&P is smaller, we feel sympathy for Mom and Pop when they lose, but no real joy for Walmart stockholders when they earn a slightly larger dividend (even if our pension fund owns stock in Walmart).

If we broaden our perspective to include the gains for the consumers, then we may have a more benign view of the process. The consumer must be gaining something when he or she shifts from M&P to Walmart. This gain may be from lower prices or from better products or service. In any case, when consumers voluntarily switch, they are gaining consumer surplus from the transaction. Thus, the first-order effect is the switch in revenue from M&P to Walmart, which may be zero-sum, but if we add in the additional consumer surplus, then the switch is overall positive-sum. This is a necessary implication of the fundamental principle discussed earlier: voluntary transactions are efficient and benefit both parties.

If we read in the paper that Walmart "outcompeted" M&P and put them out of business, then we feel sorry for M&P. But if we realize that Walmart did a better job of cooperating with consumers—that it out-cooperated M&P—then we may have a more benign view of the transaction, and of Walmart.

Pie Economics Again

Zero-sum thinking leads to focusing on the division of income or wealth rather than the size of income. In fact, because arguments and disputes over the division are often contentious and expensive, the outcome may actually be negative-sum. More importantly, however, in focusing on the division of a fixed sum, we may lose track of incentives for increasing the size of the pie in the future. Short-term division of a fixed sum has important implications for incentives for future behavior, but if we assume the pie is fixed, then we do not pay adequate attention to these future incentives.

A good example is taxation. Voters and consumers generally approach tax policy as if it deals with division of a fixed (negative) sum, the amount of revenue to be raised. This is a zero-sum view of the issue: If revenue is fixed and I pay more taxes, then you pay less. However, tax policy does not only raise revenue. It also affects incentives. For example, if business is taxed at a higher rate, there will be less investment and so less growth in the economy. Other implications of the nonzero-sum nature of taxes are discussed below.

The difference between zero-sum thinking and positive-sum thinking also translates into a difference in behavior with respect to time. If the world is zero-sum, then time is irrelevant; if something is fixed, then it does not change over time. However, if the world may be positive-sum, then time becomes important because incentives created now will affect income in the future. Returning to the taxation example, if lower business taxes increase investment, then in the future, income will be higher. But if income is fixed and unchanging (zero-sum), then there are no incentive effects and no reason to consider the long-term results of different policies. In this sense, zero-sum thinking is equivalent to short-term thinking.

We see an example in the economic policies of Western Europe. One policy was to create a good deal of job security. It became difficult to fire a worker. For employed workers, this was fine, and it raised their real incomes significantly. But there was a longer-term effect as well. Employers knew that if they hired a worker, it would be difficult in the future to fire this worker should it become profitable to do so, either because of market conditions or because the worker turned out not to be a good fit for the job. As a result, hiring decreased, and the unemployment rate for young workers increased significantly. If the number of jobs were fixed (zero-sum), this effect would not occur: Employers would hire the workers they needed. It is only because employers can vary the number of workers hired that the negative implications of worker protection laws become important, and as more time passes, the effects become larger as firms adapt.

I claimed earlier that zero-sum thinking is probably the major fallacy in noneconomists' thinking about the economy. I now provide some additional examples of fallacious zero-sum thinking, with some corrections. (For a related analysis, see Boyer and Peterson, 2018.)

Immigration and Jobs

It is often thought that immigrants take jobs from Americans. This might be so if the number of jobs were fixed, if jobs existed in a zero-sum world. But they do not. A little thought indicates that immigrants not only work, but they also consume. They work to earn money to buy food, clothing, shelter, and all the myriad goods that Americans buy. But, of course, someone must produce those goods, and those people also have jobs. So as immigrants increase consumption, they create jobs.

Indeed, immigration is positive-sum: Gains from immigration are greater than losses. This is because of the important economic principle of comparative advantage. Immigrants are better than native-born Americans at some things, and by allowing immigrants to do those things and allowing native-born Americans to do the things they are better at, everyone can gain. This is a classic example of gains from trade through cooperation. If immigrants produce the things they are better at producing (or that Americans are worse at producing, or unwilling to produce at current market prices), then prices for those goods are reduced, and Americans can purchase more goods and services, again leading to an increase in employment and in overall welfare.

For example, assume that Mexican workers can do construction work at a lower cost than Americans (apparently a realistic assumption). Then several things happen if we allow immigrants to do this work. First, of course, American workers who were engaged in construction do lose their jobs. This is where zero-sum or first-order thinking stops. Mexicans gain work, Americans lose jobs, causing unemployment. This is also where the union representing the American workers stops. But this is only the first-order effect of the immigration. Zero-sum thinking ignores second-order effects.

Here is one second-order effect. The Mexican workers get paid and they spend their earnings. Americans then get jobs producing the things that the workers are buying: maybe more workers in Chipotle, maybe more clerks in Walmart. But the spending by the immigrants will itself create some jobs to replace any jobs lost in the construction industry.

Here is another second-order effect: The immigrants were hired exactly because they are cheaper than Americans, and so costs and prices of buildings will decrease. Because of the work of the immigrants, the cost and so the price of housing will be lower than otherwise. That means that Americans buying or renting houses or condos or offices will spend less on housing, and so have more money to spend on other goods and services, increasing employment in those sectors.

Blaming immigrants for unemployment is a classic example of zero-sum thinking. The fundamental cause of the misperception is looking only at one side of the market, the production side, which looks like there is competition, and so it appears to be zero-sum. Immigrants produce, but they also consume. Moreover, in producing, immigrants cause goods to be available at lower prices, freeing resources to purchase additional goods. If we include the consumption side of the market, where cooperation occurs, then we see that immigration leads to positive-sum interactions. If we view Mexicans as competing with Americans, then we emphasize the zero-sum nature of the transaction. But if we view Mexicans as being better at cooperating with builders than are Americans, then we can more easily focus on the positive-sum nature of the transaction.

Labor Market Regulations

A related belief has to do with minimum wages and other regulations in the labor market. If the number of jobs is fixed, minimum wage laws and other regulations, such as laws mandating comparable worth (attempting to equalize earnings for men and women) will appear to serve only to transfer income (redistribute the pie); they will seem to have no effect on employment rates. But since the world is not zero-sum, these laws do have effects on employment. Minimum wages reduce employment, especially among the young and the poor. Laws such as those mandating comparable worth for wages between men and women lead to fewer women being hired. The same argument applies to laws making it more difficult to fire undesired workers. If it is more difficult to fire a worker, then employers respond by reducing hiring.

There are often parties in an economy with an interest in promoting inefficient laws, such as minimum wage laws. In positive-sum (efficient) transactions, gainers gain more than losers lose. But there *are* losers, and they have an incentive to emphasize the zero-sum nature of the transaction and try to block it. For example, union members (who all make more than minimum wages) gain when competitors (lower-paid workers) are priced out of the market by minimum wage laws. Most people don't think much about minimum wages, and when they do, they feel sorry for low-wage workers, without considering employment effects, because of zero-sum thinking. Thus, those with an economic interest in legislation can gain allies among those who don't pay much attention to the issue and don't see the harmful effects because of zero-sum thinking. Similar arguments apply to tariffs where naïve voters can be convinced by those who gain from tariffs that jobs of fellow Americans are at stake. Farmers can get price supports through the same sort of arguments. Those with an interest in promoting these laws will use the beliefs of naïve citizens in lobbying. This is made easier because of zero-sum thinking.

This effect has been called the "bootleggers and Baptists" effect (Smith and Yandle, 2014). In the South, bootleggers had an economic interest in closing the liquor stores on Sundays because they could sell their liquor on Sundays while the liquor stores were closed. Baptists also wanted the liquor stores closed because this might lead to more people going to church. Thus, there was an alliance between those with an economic interest in closing liquor stores and those who viewed the closure as a moral good. Similarly, workers with an interest in pricing their competitors out of business (the "bootleggers" in this analogy) form an alliance with misinformed but kindhearted voters who think a higher minimum wage will help the poor.

Imports

A similar analysis applies to imports and international trade. Again, in a zero-sum world, if we bought more stuff from China or India, then we would produce less stuff ourselves and some workers would become unemployed. But there are several offsetting effects.

First are exports: If we export stuff to India and China, or to other countries, then Americans produce these goods. These Americans have jobs. Second is the same price effect we saw with respect to immigrants. Since we buy imported goods, they are cheaper than domestically produced goods, so consumers gain and have more money to use purchasing additional goods, which must be produced by workers.

Indeed, with respect to international trade, the normal political discussions get it exactly backward. When we trade with other countries, they send us stuff (goods) and we send them stuff. These transfers involve money, but it is important to focus on the goods themselves—the real stuff—not on the money involved. The *benefit* of trade is the stuff they send us. That is, if they send us stuff—cars, shirts, TVs, computers—then we have more stuff. The *cost* is the stuff we need to send them. That is, if we send them stuff, then we have less stuff for ourselves. (If they are willing to accept paper, like the Chinese, we are even better off: we got the stuff, they got paper.)

Part of the problem is our focus on competition. We view Chinese manufacturers as competing with American manufacturers, and we root for the Americans, the home team. We sometimes even use a stronger negative-sum metaphor: we refer to "trade wars." But if we focused on the cooperative side of the transaction, we would see that Chinese producers are cooperating with American consumers who purchase their products, and, since the transactions are voluntary, both sides can be expected to gain. Moreover, simple economic analysis shows that the gains to American consumers from international trade are greater than the losses to American producers, so international trade is a positive-sum interaction.

Of course, firms and workers in industries that compete with imports have incentives to encourage such zero-sum beliefs in lobbying for protection. However, the lobbying is made easier because of the intuitive belief in the fixed number of jobs. That is, it is easier to obtain legislation that is consistent with zero-sum beliefs. For a while, economists seemed to have mainly won the battle over tariffs (except for especially powerful interest groups) in that tariffs were continually reduced over a long period of time. However, as discussed above, President Trump ran and won on an explicitly zero-sum or negative-sum view of trade, and this may be translated into higher tariffs (although there is some evidence that he is actually seeking a zero-tariff world, a tremendous positive-sum move).

Once again, we are misled by zero-sum thinking.

Taxation

Zero-sum thinking focuses on the distribution of taxes, not the incentive effects. This is because in a zero-sum world the only effect of taxation is to redistribute payments of money. For example, there is evidence that the public believes that taxes are too high, but also that business gets too many tax breaks, so the implication is that voters believe that personal taxes are too high and business taxes too low. Business taxes are not perceived as affecting individuals, as would be consistent with zero-sum thinking. In reality, of course, "businesses" cannot pay any taxes—all business taxes are paid by humans as owners of capital through lower returns, workers through lower wages, or consumers through higher prices. Moreover, the distribution among these parties is complex and due to market forces, not to law. Law can mandate who writes the check for a particular tax, but the actual weight of the tax is determined by markets, not by law. But zero-sum thinking causes us to look at the check writer and ignore the secondary effects, such as higher prices, lower wages, and lower dividends. These results follow from business taxation, but they are second- and third-order effects and so ignored by zero-sum thinking.

When I began writing this, President Trump had just announced the outline of a new tax plan. An Associated Press article about the plan headlined, "Trump Advisers Insist Tax Cut Proposal Will Not Favor the Rich" (Colvin, 2017). The entire article is then about the distributional effects of the tax plan. Nothing is mentioned about the effects of the tax revision (which was major) on incentives or on the size of the pie. In fact, the tax plan has passed and the second-order effects have turned out to be very large, with significant increases in employment and labor force participation, and in wages.

For another example, consider Social Security taxes. In an effort to hide the true cost of these taxes, government mandates that half be "paid" by workers and half by businesses. But labor economists know that, from the perspective of an employer, it does not matter who writes the check. In fact, all of the taxes are borne by labor. In making hiring decisions, an employer does not care if he or she pays the money directly to a worker in the form of wages or to the government for Social Security; the effect is the same. Similar analysis applies to medical insurance, including that mandated by Obamacare.

"Static" revenue analysis, which assumes that all decisions remain the same if taxes change (as sometimes used by government agencies to project effects of tax changes), is based on the same sort of zero-sum thinking. With respect to public spending, as on a subsidy, the effect will be viewed as reducing individual costs of some good or service with no implication for amount demanded. This is why *ex ante* estimates of costs of medical insurance programs and many other programs routinely underestimate these costs. The first-order effect of the subsidy will be to reduce costs for the beneficiaries, but the second-order effects will be to increase the number of people competing for the subsidy. In the case of medical care, the initial estimates were based on the amount of medical care being used by the beneficiaries—the amount they "needed." But if the cost is reduced, the law of demand comes into play, and people begin to use much more medical care.

Inequality

Anyone who pays any attention to the news must realize that there is a huge policy debate about inequality and the distribution of income. Many distinguished economists are participants in this debate. Issues related to income inequality are direct implications of zero-sum thinking. There are several important points.

Increasing inequality in income is caused by two factors: increased relative earnings by the rich, and reduced relative earnings by the poor. Change in either of these variables will lead to increased inequality. But they are unrelated. Earnings of high-income individuals can increase while earnings of low-income individuals increase, decrease, or remain the same. The only reason we think of them as related is because of zero-sum thinking. That is, if we think that there is some fixed amount of income to be divided between the rich and the poor, then if the earnings of the rich increase, the earnings of the poor must necessarily decrease. But there is no fixed amount of income to distribute, so this reasoning is wrong.

Income is not "divided" or "distributed"; it is earned. There is no pot of income to be divided among the citizens of a society. (This is where the pie metaphor breaks down.) Rather, individuals make choices about work and allocation of resources that they control, and these choices lead to earning of incomes. The fallacy of assuming a division of a fixed sum of income is an example of the belief in a zero-sum world. In a zero-sum world, there would indeed be a pot of income to divide. But in the actual nonzero-sum world in which we live, the amount of income for each individual is determined by the decisions of that individual operating in a market. Different decisions can lead to different outcomes, and different policies will lead to different decisions.

A fear of inequality can quickly become demonization of the wealthy, as we saw with protests against the 1 percent. That is, many protesters were opposed to the rich, on the assumption that because they were rich, others were poor. This attitude is consistent with a world in which the rich become rich by taking from the poor: a zero-sum world. In fact, economics teaches us that individual earnings are approximately equal to each individual's "marginal revenue product," the additional contribution of a worker to earnings of the employer. This means that as a first approximation, differences in earnings are due to differences in productivity, and those with higher earnings are simply more productive. Moreover, the total product created by an individual (whether a worker or an investor) is greater than the marginal product, so that higher-earning individuals also contribute more to society. In other words, richer individuals are rich because they have produced a lot and, while they get some of the increased value of their productivity, much of it goes to others. Bill Gates and Steve Jobs became very rich in the computer business, but the value (consumer surplus) to all of us of their contributions was vastly greater than the amount they and their investors and employees received for themselves. If we increase taxes on the wealthy, they will respond in some way—perhaps working less, perhaps investing in less risky but lower-expected-return activities. Of course, the private return is what motivates individuals to create social value, but the social value itself is a benefit to the rest of us.

Although economists distinguish between capital and labor, in reality it is impossible to separate them because all workers have embedded in themselves some human capital. Some of this human capital is innate, some is acquired in school, and some on the job, but a wage includes a payment both for the labor provided by the worker and for the human capital involved. Moreover, the human capital component of the wage is much larger for most workers (approximately, those earning above the minimum wage) than is the labor component. Thus, it is not meaningful to distinguish between earnings of labor and of capital.

Workers and owners of capital make choices about allocation of their labor and capital. Any attempt to use the tax system to reduce inequality will lead to different choices. Higher taxes on labor will lead some to work less, or to retire earlier, or to take easier or more pleasant but lower-paying jobs. Investors will also skew their investments in response to taxes, perhaps by investing in safer but less productive alternatives. After all, if the government takes part of the profits but the investor himself bears all the losses, then risk-taking becomes less desirable. Therefore, any effort to redistribute income will also have the effect of reducing the total amount of income in society, and the amount which might be redistributed. Reduced incomes will lead to reduced economic growth, and so will harm even the poor in the long run. As discussed above, society must determine the terms of the trade-off between fairness and efficiency. We cannot arbitrarily mandate some distribution of income with no effects on the size of total income. The notion that we can is an example of zero-sum thinking.

What should concern us is the level of incomes of the poor and middle class, not the pattern of incomes by class. To increase the incomes of lower-income people, we should adopt policies which increase their opportunities, and refrain from policies that reduce these opportunities. For example, minimum wages reduce entry-level jobs, and for those workers who are hired, there is less on-the-job training. For both of these reasons, it is more difficult for low-wage workers to move to the middle class. Of course, in a zero-sum world neither of these effects would occur, so many ignore them in thinking about policy. The real danger from focusing on inequality is that it leads to a static view of the economy. The only way to benefit people in the long run is to focus on economic growth, and paying attention to inequality leads us in exactly the wrong direction. Size-of-the-pie effects are much more important than distribution of the pie.

The zero-sum view of business and of wealth acquisition may explain the way business is portrayed in movies and fiction. Ribstein (2012) shows that movies generally portray business in a negative light. A specific example is from the 1987 movie *Wall Street*, in which a financier engaged in efficiently moving assets from lower- to higher-valued uses by closing an inefficient plant is depicted as evil. If the world is zero-sum, then wealth is limited, and if the main way to be wealthy is to take money from others, then attitudes viewing the wealthy as evil could be part of our mental architecture. This is consistent with some religious beliefs: consider Jesus saying that "It is easier for a camel to pass through the eye of a needle than for a rich man to enter the kingdom of God" (Matthew 19:24). Ayn Rand did portray businessmen in a favorable light, but her novels and movies based on them, while appealing to a subset of people, have not been major popular successes. (Her novels are also very long. Perhaps if they had been shorter, more people would have read them.)

An interesting exception might appear to be Horatio Alger, a very successful nineteenth-century author who wrote many popular "rags to riches" books about poor boys who became rich and successful. Indeed, when someone is very successful, we still sometimes refer to a

"Horatio Alger tale." But careful reading of these novels indicates that the boys became successful by providing some benefit to a wealthy individual, such as finding and returning a lost sum of money. The wealthy man (always) then takes the poor boy as a ward. Notice that the boy's wealth is not earned in a productive way; it is transferred from a benefactor. In other words, there is no wealth creation in Horatio Alger stories, and they are consistent with a zero-sum world.

If we focus too much on "fairness," we can also cause waste, because we may neglect efficiency. This will generally be the result of zero-sum thinking. Here is an example: In New York City, builders of condominiums in Manhattan must sometimes make some units available at a below-market price to lower-income individuals because of some notion of fairness. The argument is based on the notion that the number of units is fixed, and allocating some of them to lower-income individuals will be purely redistributive. But in fact, forcing landlords to sell some units at below-market prices will reduce the profit from building, and the result is that fewer apartments overall will be built. If we want to force developers to subsidize low-income individuals, a better alternative would be a direct tax, which could then be used to purchase a larger number of less-expensive apartments for lower-income persons in less-expensive areas. More generally, it is not clear why developers (or purchasers of new apartments, who will actually pay any tax) should be the ones to subsidize housing for low-income persons. If we want such a subsidy, then all taxpayers should pay for it.

Marxism

Marxist theory is fundamentally incorrect. Economists have known this based on theoretical reasoning for a long time, and the collapse of the Soviet Union, or more recently of Venezuela, as a result of the most important social science experiment in history is further evidence of its basic errors. Consider also the difference between East and West Germany or North and South Korea, where in both cases the

Marxist entity is or has been poor and miserable, and the capitalist entity rich and prosperous. Nonetheless, in spite of the clear theoretical and empirical failure of Marxist thought, many people agreed with the tenants of Marxism, and many, including many otherwise smart academics, still do. The reason is that Marxism is basically consistent with zero-sum thinking. Marx claimed to have an advanced science of history and a theory of "scientific socialism." That is, Marx claimed that this theory of class conflict and economic determinism placed socialism on a firm scientific foundation. In fact, Marxist economics is based on our incorrect intuition about economics; it is primitive, not scientific. The theory draws on primitive notions of economics, on "folk economics." Moreover, Marxism is fundamentally an economic theory. Since the economics is demonstrably wrong, other implications, such as "alienation" or the focus on "race, class, gender" used by scholars in the humanities, cannot be correct.

Perhaps the essence of Marxist thinking is in the aphorism, "From each according to his ability, to each according to his needs." This statement is fundamentally based on a zero-sum view of the world. Each clause reflects a zero-sum error.

"From each according to his ability" implies that each person produces a fixed amount, based on his or her productivity. But the amount that a person actually produces depends in a deep sense on incentives. In the short run (the immediate period), the amount someone produces depends on how hard he or she works and on what level of risks he or she is willing to accept, which in turn depends on issues such as wages and taxes. As wages go up or taxes go down, people work harder and take greater risks, and produce more. Of course, people with more "ability" will produce more per hour than people with less ability, but the amount they produce will not in any sense be fixed. More specifically, if we allocate output independently of productivity (so that more productive people get no more than others with the same "needs"), then the total amount produced by an economy will be greatly reduced.

Moreover, in the long run, the effect of ignoring incentives will be greater. In the short run, the skills and training of workers is fixed, but in the longer period, people can decide how much to invest in acquiring skills. We might all like to major in art, music, and literature in college (if we go at all), since looking at great art, listening to music, and reading great books is more fun for most people than studying accounting or chemistry, but many of us study less interesting subjects because they will lead to higher incomes. Many also go to even more boring graduate schools because of the extra earnings available from a graduate or professional degree. If we decouple earnings from productivity, people will be less likely to acquire valuable skills, which will further reduce the size of the economy in the long run.

The second part of the aphorism, "to each according to his needs," is also an example of zero-sum thinking. It assumes that "needs" are fixed and can be ascertained. But the most fundamental principle of economics is the law of demand, which says that the amount of anything we consume is determined by price. It is not possible to measure needs independent of price. Moreover, if we did try to allocate income based on needs, this would itself have harmful effects. For example, a family with more children "needs" more money than a family with fewer, so we would create a false incentive for people to have children. A broken family needs more money than an intact family, so we would create an incentive for family breakdown. Indeed, many of our welfare laws have created exactly these incentives. In general, social pathologies create more needs, so the Marxist prescription would create more social pathologies. If we subsidize something, perhaps by greater payments for the needs created, then we will get more of it.

Of course, since the first part (from each according to his ability) is incorrect, if we try to allocate output based on needs and not on productivity, there will be so little produced that we would return to a subsistence economy, and we might begin allocating resources only to avoid starvation. But this state of affairs is not one we should seek to attain. Zero-sum thinking leads to a belief that variables like skills, training, hours of work, types of jobs, risk-taking, and family size are fixed, but like most or all economic variables, these things respond to prices and other incentives.

There is another aspect of primitive economic thinking in Marxism. One of the great counterintuitive lessons of economics is that the uncoordinated plans of millions of individuals can lead to an efficient outcome. This notion is alien to folk economics. Moreover, because of the primacy of political over economic thinking, it is natural to think of the economy as requiring central direction for it to function. To many, the invisible hand is not only invisible, but it is also nonexistent.

Therefore, in running a Marxist economy, the state determines prices and quantities. However, because fundamental laws of economics are ignored, the prices and the quantities chosen are not linked to one another through markets, and so the plans are inconsistent. Incentives are not aligned. As a result, a centrally planned economy does not work. This is the ultimate explanation for the collapse of the Soviet economy and for the great levels of poverty exhibited by the existing planned economies, North Korea, Cuba, and Venezuela. They all suffer the consequences of attempting to legislate an economy based on zero-sum thinking. Since the collapse of the Venezuelan economy is very recent and ongoing, it should serve as a lesson to those favoring a socialist regime in the U.S. and elsewhere.

Additionally, a centrally planned and centrally run economy requires a large government sector to run it. This means that the government acquires a lot of power. If the people realize that electing a communist government was an error, it is difficult or impossible to correct that error using democratic voting because of the entrenched power of the bureaucracy. This is why, for example, Cuba and

Venezuela are now in deep economic trouble but nonetheless unable to democratically change their circumstances.

Other aspects of Marxism also reflect zero-sum thinking. The notion of class warfare between capital and labor (or, in neo-Marxism, among races, classes, and genders) assumes that there is a fixed sum to be divided and that if capital or men or white people get more, then labor or women or black people get less. (As discussed in Chapter 1, this is also an example of primitive "us versus them" thinking.) This ignores the basic cooperation between factors or groups needed to produce output in the first place. Output is produced by labor and capital working together. Labor is more productive as it has more capital with which to work (a man with a shovel can produce more than a man with a spoon, but less than a man with a tractor), and moreover, most workers in an advanced society already incorporate a lot of human capital, so it is not even possible to separate labor from capital. There may be some conflict over the division of the surplus, but the big point is that the cooperation of labor and capital generates a huge surplus in the first place. A capitalist economy is so productive exactly because it puts capital and labor together in the most productive way.

There are two additional fundamental fallacies in Marxist thought. One is that members of a "class" with millions of members, such as capitalists or whites or men, can agree to exploit and underpay labor or blacks or women, even though it would be in each of their individual interests to cheat on such an agreement. The other is the "labor theory of value," that all value comes from labor and none from capital. This is consistent with our mental architecture which evolved in a world of little capital. Since these fallacies are less closely related to zero-sum thinking, I will not discuss them here.

Law

There are two fundamental parts of law: criminal law and civil law. Criminal law is more "fun," so there are more books and TV shows dealing with criminal law than with private disputes between individuals, the stuff of civil law. But civil law has much more relevance to our day-to-day lives for most of us than does criminal law. I will first discuss civil law, and then briefly discuss criminal law, with an emphasis on zero-sum thinking.

We think of law as comprising lawsuits, and these seem to be the essence of negative-sum, noncooperative arrangements, since both parties must pay legal fees, and so the amount the winner gets is less than the amount the loser pays. But recent analysis indicates that there are a lot of cooperative positive-sum aspects to law. Law is not a zero-sum pursuit. As traditionally understood, the purpose of private (noncriminal) law was redistribution: zero-sum. If I broke a contract with you, you sued me for damages, and the amount I paid was equal to the amount you lost from my breach. Actually, of course, we both had legal fees, so the interaction between us was negative-sum, but it was still a redistributive event.

Similar analysis would have applied to harm from an accident (tort law). If I harmed you, I would pay you the costs you incurred. If we had a dispute over property, then the court would decide who had the property right, using legal principles. In all of these cases, the law was viewed as if the purpose was to determine winners and losers, and to distribute what was viewed as a fixed sum between them, again subtracting legal fees. Fundamentally, since law was invoked after something bad happened (a contract breach, an accident, a trespass) then all the law could do was allocate the costs and benefits of this action. That is, law was viewed as being "ex post" (after the event). The costs of the legal harm (the contract breach, the accident) were "sunk," and a fundamental principle of economics is that sunk costs are irrelevant for decision-making.

The Law and Economics revolution, due mainly to Richard Posner (1973/2014), replaced this zero-sum view of the law with a positive-sum view of the law. Part of Posner's insight was that the law was actually concerned with efficiency (positive-sum events), but the judges spoke as if they were concerned with distribution (zero-sum events). The law did not merely redistribute losses from past events. It created incentives for future behavior, and those incentives could be structured to lead to "efficient" (positive-sum) behaviors. For example, it will sometimes be efficient for a party to break a contract. If I can break my contract and pay you as much as you would have made had I not breached, and still come out ahead, then it is efficient for me to break the contract. If payments for breach (called "damages" in the law) are correctly chosen, then I will break my contract if and only if it is efficient for me to do so. In this simple case, the amount I should pay you for breach is the "benefit of the bargain," the amount you would make if I kept the contract. If I can pay you that amount and still come out ahead, then breach is efficient because I am ahead, and you are no worse off.

Similar principles apply to the other areas of private law. If payments for harms caused by accidents are correctly structured, then potential victims (say, pedestrians) and potential injurers (say, drivers) will both have incentives to be optimally careful. Optimally careful does not mean maximally careful. Pedestrians will cross streets and drivers will drive on those streets at speeds of more than five miles per hour. But both parties will take the right amount of care—say, drivers will drive at the speed limit and pedestrians will look both ways before crossing. Properly determined damages can create incentives for exactly this sort of efficient behavior.

If we have a dispute over some property right, then again, the law can resolve this dispute in the most efficient way, generally by attempting to determine which of us puts a higher value on the right. For example, your nightclub makes noise and keeps me awake. The court must decide who has a right to "quiet." If the court determines that the value to you of the nightclub is greater than the lost value of all of the affected homeowners, it may grant the property right to "quiet" to the nightclub. If the value to the homeowners is greater, then the court will order the nightclub to be quiet. More complex solutions are also possible: The nightclub can make noise until 11:00 p.m. and then it must stop. Again, the court is trying to maximize the joint value between the two parties: it is trying to achieve a positive-sum outcome. (A very important result in law and economics, the "Coase theorem," says that if costs of negotiation are low enough, the parties can renegotiate the right if the courts get it wrong.)

The law still sometimes makes errors, based on zero-sum thinking. Modern American product liability and medical malpractice law can best be understood as if jurors and others believe that the only effect of a judgment is to redistribute wealth from businesses or physicians, or their insurance companies, to injured consumers, with no effects on investment, production, or prices. This, of course, is zero-sum thinking. In fact, law creates incentives for behavior. The purpose of liability law is to compensate victims and to prevent future harmful behavior. However, these laws may in fact be counterproductive because of the incentives created. For example, excess malpractice liability can lead to physicians avoiding treatments that may lead to litigation. There is evidence that in some cases, modern tort law has gone too far in protecting consumers, and some of the incentives for accident avoidance are so great that cutting back on the law (what is called "tort reform") can actually increase safety and reduce fatalities (Rubin and Shepherd, 2007).

Malpractice law provides another example of zero-sum thinking. Physicians often complain that their malpractice insurance premiums are too high, perhaps as high as $200,000 for some specialties, such as obstetricians. Doctors act as if their incomes would be higher if they did not have to pay these premiums. But in reality, some or all of the cost of malpractice insurance is built into the cost of medical care. If insurance premiums were lower, then fees for delivering babies would also be lower, and incomes of obstetricians would be lower. While doctors may pay some of the cost of malpractice insurance, patients (through paying for their own health insurance) pay most of them.

Another example is from antitrust law. It is commonly believed that predatory pricing (pricing to drive a rival out of business in order to become a monopolist) is commonplace and a normal business tactic. This notion is related to zero-sum thinking since in a zero-sum world the only way for one firm to grow is to take business from others. In fact, both theory and evidence demonstrate that predatory pricing is very uncommon. It is much cheaper to purchase a rival than to drive him out of business, because the predator (being larger and selling more at below-cost prices) actually loses more money than does the victim. However, for many years, the antitrust laws acted as if predation was common.

Untrained individuals also believe that monopoly is much more common than economists believe it is. Survey evidence indicates that noneconomists are much more likely than economists to believe that business profits are too high, that top executives are paid too much, that greed of oil companies explained the "recent" (whenever it has happened, the same cause is assumed) rise in gasoline prices, and that the price of gasoline is too high. This survey finds that the mean estimate by the public of profit rates on sales is 46.7 percent, while the correct value is 3 percent. A popular topic for policy debate is the pricing of pharmaceuticals; this debate proceeds as if profitability had no effect on research or on the amount of innovation in the industry.

I have so far considered private law. But zero-sum thinking is also relevant for understanding some aspects of criminal law. Attitudes toward crime may be influenced by zero-sum thinking. Glorification of some criminals (Robin Hood, the Godfather, the Sopranos, my favorite, Raymond Reddington of *Blacklist*) may be easier in a world where the only effect of crime is viewed as redistribution; in reality, of course, crime leads to reallocation of resources and reductions of real incomes as people take measures to avoid victimization costs.

Moreover, when we think of jail or other punishments, we view these as being "deserved." However, this is an example of zero-sum thinking. The purpose of criminal punishment is to deter future criminal behavior. What should be relevant in deciding on punishment is the effect on deterring future criminals. But zero-sum thinking leads us to believe that the amount of crime is fixed, and so deterrence is not relevant.

Noneconomic Implications of Zero-Sum Thinking

So far, I have discussed the economic implications of zero-sum thinking. However, there are additionally noneconomic costs of such thinking, and the noneconomic costs may in fact be much greater than the economic costs. Indeed, zero-sum thinking may be one of the most harmful errors known to humanity.

Racism and Its Relatives

Racist behavior is based on zero-sum thinking. The underlying belief is that something is fixed and if blacks or Jews or some other group gets more, then some other group must get less. This sort of thinking is similar to thinking about immigrants. Indeed, to the extent that immigrants are from a different racial or ethnic group, it is the same thinking. In fact, as Nobel laureate Gary Becker showed in his early work in discrimination, if there is racial discrimination against some group (say, blacks) in an economy by some other group (say, whites), blacks and whites both lose from this discrimination. This is because discrimination acts like a tariff: It reduces trade between the groups. Like any tariff, there are gainers and losers in both groups, but the net effect of discrimination is to make both groups worse off. (Blacks lose more than whites, in this example, but both lose.) In our terms, discrimination reduces cooperation between groups, and reducing cooperation also reduces incomes.

Consider a world in which capital and labor work together cooperatively to produce output. Assume that blacks have more labor per capita than whites, and whites have more capital. If there is free trade (no discrimination), then labor from blacks will combine with capital from whites to produce output. If there is discrimination, then capital from whites will have less labor to work with because it cannot work with black labor, and so the return on capital owned by whites will be reduced. Similarly, labor from blacks will have less capital to work with, and so its return will be reduced. On the other hand, labor from whites will have more capital to use, and so its return will increase. Similarly, capital from blacks will have more labor to work with (because black labor cannot work with white capital) and so will have a higher return. So reducing discrimination will lead to redistribution from black capital and white labor to black labor and white capital. But overall the gains to those who gain from eliminating discrimination will be larger than the losses to those who lose from eliminating discrimination. Allowing more cooperation will lead to increased overall output.

Note that this analysis turns a Marxist-inspired story of "exploitation" on its head. In the Marxist view, capitalists gain from discrimination by exploiting minorities. In fact, it is labor that gains from discrimination and capital that loses. This is consistent with the facts. Labor unions were traditionally among the major sources of racial discrimination. A major blow to discrimination in the U.S. was the migration of capital in the form of white-owned manufacturing businesses (initially mainly textile) from the Northeast to the South. These migrating businesses were willing to hire black workers, thus increasing the workers' opportunities and wages, and increasing the capital owners' return. Similarly, in South Africa under apartheid, mine owners (white capitalists) wanted to promote black miners, and it was white mine workers who were opposed to these promotions.

At the limit, racism becomes genocide. Again, the theory is based on zero-sum thinking. If "we" can eliminate the Armenians or the Jews or the Tutsi (all of whom have been targets of genocide), then there will be more for "us." This sort of reasoning ignores the basis for trade and the fact that more diversity and larger markets can lead to increased specialization and benefits for all. Our intuition is to view the nature of interracial interactions as competitive, rather than understanding that in a well-functioning world they can be cooperative. Thus, although I have stressed the economic costs of zero-sum thinking, the human costs in terms of genocide and wars is probably much greater.

A Digression: Mathematics and Teaching Economics

By some measures, this seems like a great time for the field of economics. Economists are hired at universities, in government, and increasingly in businesses, including at leading tech firms. We are well paid. Economists generally recommend little regulation, reduced taxes, and free trade, and the current (Trump) administration has adopted two and a half of these policies, with substantial economic success.

And yet, we economists have failed in a very basic regard. We are not educating students about the merits of a capitalist free market system, and we are not educating them about the costs of a socialist system. Thus, students lack basic economic literacy. This is important in a democracy because students become voters and politicians, and they do not understand the basic system they are controlling.

Economists disagree on the scope of the optimal role of government in society. But virtually all mainstream economists agree that a socialist system, where government controls the means of production in most important segments of the economy, is vastly less efficient than a capitalist economy. If theory were not enough to teach this lesson, we continually have real-world examples, with Venezuela being the most recent. Nonetheless, as discussed above, many Americans support socialism and prefer it to capitalism.

Some of the most fervent supporters of socialism are college students—and at most universities, capitalism is a dirty word. The young people supporting socialism are our students, and we economists should teach them the problems with this fashionable but flawed

75

economic system. But most students do not take economics, and those who do take an introductory economics class may not receive such an education.

There are many reasons for this. Economists respond to incentives, and the incentive system for economists puts little weight on teaching the benefits of capitalism. Most economists, like most academics, advance their careers by publishing articles in increasingly technical and mathematical professional journals. An important result of this is that the classes we teach are becoming increasingly technical and specialized, requiring high-level mathematics. This has the effect of reducing undergraduate demand for the economics major.

It is even worse at the graduate level. I am asked once or twice a year by students who support free markets but lack math skills what to study in graduate school, and I must tell these students that without a good bit of math, it is impossible to get a PhD in economics.

I am not opposed to rigor in economics research and in policy advising. But it would be possible to teach undergraduate economics with a lower level of math. Very few of our students go on to become PhD economists; most go to business or law school, or directly to the job market. But we teach as if we are teaching future economics professors. Ordinary citizens need a basic knowledge of economics in order to vote rationally: What will be the consequences of a tax cut or increase? What is the effect of international trade on the economy? What are the costs and benefits of occupational licensing laws?

There are a few basic economic principles that are nonintuitive but do not require technical skills to understand. If these were more widely understood, then markets would be viewed more favorably, and socialism would lose its appeal. A very important distinction is the difference between the size of the pie (the amount of goods and services produced) and the division of the pie (who gets how much). Economics focuses on the size of the pie—how can society's scarce resources be used to produce the most efficient bundle of goods and services?

Voters often focus on the division of the pie—who gets how much? This is because untrained people often view the world as zero-sum. Indeed, zero-sum thinking is probably the cause of most errors in economic thinking, including a belief in socialism. Economies can grow, and it is possible for the rich to get richer at the same time that the poor get richer. The common homily, "The rich get richer and the poor get poorer" is neither certain nor sure; it is totally contrary to fact in a growing market economy

The most basic premise of economics is that hundreds of millions of people can interact with one another with no central direction and no coordination, and yet can reach a consistent outcome which itself has certain efficient properties. This is Adam Smith's famous "invisible hand." Because this is not widely understood, there are frequent calls for central direction and central planning, despite its massive failure in the Soviet Union, Venezuela, and wherever else it has been tried.

Economists also understand that selfish behavior can nonetheless lead to desirable outcomes. The uncoordinated behavior can be motivated by selfish ends, and yet the outcome will generally be efficient. Motives do not matter; outcomes do. In some sense, we are all out to maximize our incomes, but the way to do this in a market economy is to provide something that others want to buy. Steve Jobs and Bill Gates became fantastically wealthy by creating the computer revolution, and their financial wealth was only a small part of the massive social wealth they created. In a socialist economy, the way to gain wealth is to gain power over others.

If we economists would make the effort to teach these points to as many students as possible, we could reduce the demand by voters for a socialistic economy. Perhaps donors or foundations supporting free markets could create a system of prizes for economists who advance the understanding of markets for ordinary citizens. This could reorder incentives and lead to more and better teaching, and perhaps better economic policy.

CHAPTER 3

COOPERATION

My purpose in this book is twofold. I want to convince you that it is improper to characterize a free market economy as "competitive," and I want to convince you that it is proper to characterize such an economy as "cooperative." In this chapter I will analyze the cooperative nature of a market economy. There are roles for both cooperation and competition in a free economy, but I want to argue that pride of place should belong to cooperation. A secondary argument is that focusing on the competitive aspect of a market economy leads to a bias against the capitalist system, which is itself harmful.

Coordinated and Uncoordinated

We may think of two types of cooperation, which I will call coordinated, or planned cooperation, and uncoordinated, or unplanned cooperation. Business firms and indeed all economic institutions are examples of planned or coordinated cooperation. Coordinated cooperation is what we observe in organizations such as firms or universities or government bureaus: Someone (the CEO of the firm, the president of the university, the head of the bureau) controls the organization, acquires resources (including hiring workers and raising money), and generally directs the organization toward some goal. Individuals who choose to work for this organization then consciously cooperate to reach this goal, generally because they are paid for doing so.

Uncoordinated cooperation occurs when individuals work toward some goal without consciously planning to work together. Basically, uncoordinated cooperation is what occurs in markets. Markets cannot be said to have goals in the sense that organizations have goals. There is no peak manager or CEO for a market, so there is no individual who has a goal for the market. Each participant in a market is out to maximize his or her own welfare. Nonetheless, the great insight of economics is that this uncoordinated activity generally leads to certain very nice outcomes. We may characterize the outcome of the market as maximizing consumer welfare or as moving resources toward their highest-valued uses or as maximizing efficiency of resource use. The insight of economics is that uncoordinated transactions in markets which meet certain conditions (traditionally called pure competition by economists, but which I characterize as pure cooperation) lead to these nice outcomes. What I am claiming here is that we should view markets as an uncoordinated cooperative effort to achieve these goals. Because there is no coordination, we may miss the cooperative nature of markets, but it is there and it is fundamental.

There are also intermediate levels of cooperation, as when economic activity is coordinated through contracts or long-term agreements. Here, entities have their own goals and agendas, but they achieve these goals by explicitly coordinating their plans with other entities. A major method of cooperation is through specialization and its correlate, division of labor.

I now consider first uncoordinated (market) cooperation, then coordinated cooperation, cooperation through contract, and finally specialization.

Markets: Uncoordinated Cooperation

Economics is fundamentally about cooperation. Economics is about behavior in markets, and markets are a method of facilitating cooperation. When I buy something from you, we both gain; we are cooperating. This cooperation is in some sense unconscious and uncoordinated. Each of us is out to maximize our own utility or satisfaction. The cooperation is a byproduct.

Consider the following: The fundamental economic unit is the transaction and transacting (exchanging) is a cooperative act. But when I say that economics is about cooperation, I am not making any unusual assumptions about human behavior. There is a caricature in economics of the "economic man" as a selfish, rational, calculating person, like Scrooge. Behavioral economics has shown that that caricature is false; people are actually kinder and more cooperative than that caricature allows. But for my purposes we can use that picture. We can assume that people are selfish and uncaring—all Scrooges. My point is that even the perfectly selfish economic actor is highly cooperative. A selfish person will engage in lots of transactions to generate benefits for himself, and transactions are cooperative. I need not assume that people are caring, generous, altruistic, or any related New Age personality type (although people may be of this sort). My point holds even for traditional rational, selfish individuals. Indeed, even the original Scrooge engaged in transactions. It appears that he was mainly in the money lending business, which meant many cooperative transactions with borrowers. Moreover, because of his "Scrooge-like" behavior, he was able to lend more money to more deserving (efficient) users of the funds.

This point is important for economists. We pride ourselves on being hard-headed and not naïvely sentimental like some other (unnamed) social scientists. But being hard-headed and rational and even selfish does not mean that humans do not cooperate. We economists study exchange, and exchange is itself highly cooperative.

A market economy is basically cooperative. The important point about an exchange is that both parties gain. If I buy a car from you, it is because I value the car more than the money I pay you, and you value the money more than the car. If I work for Emory University, it is because Emory values my time more than the money they must pay me, and I value the money more than the time which I must devote to Emory. The logic of transactions is simple: they are voluntary, and therefore both parties must cooperate and must gain.

The first step in cooperation is that buyers and sellers must find one another. Buyers might search for sellers or sellers might search for buyers (for example, through advertising, or using Google or Craigslist or, in the past, the classified ads in a newspaper), but the search process is cooperative. Both buyers and sellers expect to gain by finding one another. Search is two-sided: Buyers want to find sellers, and sellers want to find buyers. Sellers will advertise in those venues where they are most likely to find buyers, and buyers will search in those venues where they are most likely to find goods and services that they want to purchase. The two-sided nature of search is shown by the internet. Many of the big players on the internet—Google, Facebook, Amazon, LinkedIn, eBay, Uber, Match—have grown and thrived exactly because they have taken advantage of this two-sided nature of search and created platforms where buyers and sellers can find one another. The search process is cooperative.

Once they have found each other, the next step is that both parties provide information to their potential partner. The seller will typically describe the details of the product ("It is guaranteed for five years"). The buyer will describe the details of what he or she wants to purchase ("Do you have it in red?"). They may also negotiate over details of the transaction, such as method of payment, length of guarantee, and price itself. The result of this negotiation is that the terms of the transaction are the most efficient possible set of terms. Although each party may be seeking his or her own advantage in the negotiation, the results will be efficient and thus the negotiation process leads to cooperative terms. In those cases where the parties do not negotiate, the market process itself will ensure that the terms are efficient, as discussed below.

When they do find each other and agree on what will be sold and under what terms, then they engage in a cooperative act, the transaction. When a merchant puts a product out for sale, the merchant is inviting a buyer to cooperate. The merchant will announce the proposed sale in the terms most likely to induce the sale. For example, advertising is a search for those who are most likely to buy—to engage in a cooperative act with the merchant. When a buyer does purchase the product, the cooperative act is complete.

Consider advertising in more detail. In most cases, advertising is expensive: Advertisers must pay someone to get their message across. It is in the advertisers' interest to make this spending as effective as possible—that is, to not waste money advertising to those unlikely to purchase the product. Traditionally, advertising was only weakly targeted. For example, advertisers know something about the majority of viewers of a particular TV show (say, they are middle-aged families) and would try to advertise products that would appeal to that audience.

More recently, it has become feasible to target advertising much more carefully. This is because modern advertising media, including especially the internet, allows advertisers to gather much more information about potential customers and to direct their advertising to those most likely to purchase their product. Some people take a one-sided view of advertising and believe that this targeting is solely for the benefit of the advertiser and exploits or harms consumers in some way. But if we realize that transactions are cooperative, then we can understand that both buyers and sellers benefit from a good pairing.

We can see this more clearly if we consider the behavior of potential buyers on the internet. Buyers engage in searching for sellers. Again, this was common in the past, when the Yellow Pages were used for searches. But the has made this process much more precise. Google and Amazon have made a huge amount of money, largely by putting buyers and sellers in contact and by allowing buyers to specify in great detail the products they are looking for. More generally, the internet is full of two-sided search engines which facilitate searching by buyers and sellers for one another to engage in cooperative exchange. Many people are upset because firms "target" consumers and use devices such as cookies to identify types of consumers. However, consider what this targeting means. It means that sellers try to identify consumers who are most likely to want (benefit from) their products. Advertisers are searching for the consumers who will be the best match for their products. They are seeking the consumers who can best cooperate with the seller. It is not clear why consumers should be upset about this practice since it means that they are most likely to be provided information about products they may want to buy, and indeed, most do not seem to dislike this behavior.

Of course, some transactions go bad; the car might be a lemon. But in almost all cases transactions are beneficial to both parties. A transaction is the essence of a cooperative act. Economists call the benefits of a transaction "gains from trade." These are divided between the individuals based on the price of the transaction. With higher prices sellers gain more, and with lower prices buyers gain more, but both parties gain something from the transaction or else they would not agree to it. The transaction will occur only if the buyer values the product or service more than the seller, and in this case if there is a transaction, then both parties gain.

Economics textbooks generally teach gains from trade as part of the unit on international economics. Often, they do not specify that every transaction involves gains from trade, whether it is an international transaction or a simple trade between neighbors ("You watch my kids this week, I'll watch yours next week."). Every actual transaction is positive-sum; that is, every transaction leads to gains for both parties. Indeed, this is the basis of the argument that transactions are cooperative. The basis of a market economy is that voluntary transactions benefit both parties.

Gains from trade can take many forms. In a primitive economy, based on foraging, one person may have more meat and another may have more fruit, so a trade can be beneficial. Trade can also be intertemporal (over time): I have a good hunt this week, so I give you some meat in the expectation that next week you will reciprocate if our positions are reversed.

In more advanced economies, there is still some trade between individuals. There are more goods, and so more possibilities for mutually beneficial trade. My kids are grown so I don't want such a large house; I sell it to someone with young kids. I buy a new sports car and sell the van. In recent years, the scope of direct interpersonal transactions has increased as internet-based organizations like Craigslist and eBay have greatly increased the scope of such interpersonal transactions by reducing search costs and making it easier for buyers and sellers to find one another. Other internet organizations are increasing the scope of these trades by establishing places where buyers and sellers can more easily seek one another out. These include Airbnb, which allows those with excess living space to find those willing to pay for such space, and Lyft and Uber, which do the same for space in cars. Previously, newspaper classified ads performed the same function, albeit not as well. The internet is also allowing more service transactions—websites and apps such as TaskRabbit and Fiverr enable both businesses and individuals to find others who are willing to do small jobs. Without the internet, searching for such individuals would be prohibitively costly, but the internet has enabled such markets. As we see below, this has also enabled increased specialization.

But even so, most trades in advanced economies are indirect, between individuals and organizations. I work for Emory University; that is, I trade my time as an economist with Emory, which resells this time to students who want to learn economics, or at least who want a degree which may require learning economics, or at least passing an economics exam. Students or their parents in turn get the money they pay to Emory by selling their services in other markets. I use the money I get from Emory to buy food, shelter, clothing, and the other myriad goods available in an advanced economy. I buy them from Amazon, supermarkets, drugstores, restaurants, department stores, and other economic organizations. But each of these trades and exchanges is positive-sum: Each provides benefits to both parties, else we would not voluntarily enter into the transactions. Each is cooperative.

Of course, Emory is an intermediary. The role of an intermediary is to facilitate buyers and sellers finding one another. Emory hires me, and so certifies that I am qualified to teach economics. It also selects students, certifying that they can learn at a certain level. This is valuable because the amount that I can teach to a class depends on the average level of students in that class, and so students are willing to pay more for a school with other students of about the same ability. In a sense, students at a school are cooperating with one another.

But one effect of the internet is to reduce costs of buyers and sellers finding one another, and thus reducing the value of intermediaries. Online services such as Marginal Revolution University and Coursera are enabling students and teachers to more directly find one another, and so may reduce the value of intermediaries such as Emory in the future. This has already happened with many intermediaries, such as travel agents and bookstores.

One of the conditions of a well-functioning market economy is "freedom of contract." This means that people have the right to engage in whatever deals that they themselves desire. In our terms, this means that the state does not limit the ability of people to cooperate with one another. If I am forbidden by law from certain contracts (say, by a minimum wage law or a maximum interest rate law), this simply means that there are certain potential cooperative relationships that

are made unavailable to me. If I am forbidden from hiring some practitioner (say, a specialist in drafting wills who is not an attorney, or a
dental whitening expert who is not a dentist) who is unlicensed, then
again, I am forbidden from certain sources of cooperation.

Such regulations are two-sided: they affect both consumers and
producers. For example, we usually think that a minimum wage law
forbids an employer from paying less than some amount. But it also
forbids a worker from working for less than that amount. If a worker
is worth no more than six dollars per hour because that is all the value
he or she can produce, then a minimum wage of seven dollars means
that worker cannot be hired, cannot cooperate with that employer.
Similarly, a usury (maximum interest rate) law forbids lenders from
charging high interest rates. But it also denies borrowers the right to
pay high interest rates. If a borrower is risky (has a high probability
of not repaying a loan) then a usury law may mean that person cannot
cooperate with lenders and cannot borrow money. While there may be
reasons for such laws, we should realize that they have effects on both
sides of the market. Any interference with freedom of contract limits
possibilities of cooperation for both parties.

One increasingly common form of limiting cooperation is occupational licensing. In recent years, the number of occupations which are
licensed has increased, so that it is now estimated that 30 percent of
all jobs in the U.S require a license. There are well over one thousand
categories of jobs that are licensed and in which an unlicensed person
cannot practice. The justification for these laws is generally in terms of
protecting consumers from incompetent practitioners. The argument
is that incompetents would enter and take advantage of consumers.

If we consider the cooperative nature of transactions, it is clear
that by forbidding some sellers from dealing with consumers, we are
also forbidding consumers from dealing with those sellers. It may be
that consumers would be deceived about quality of sellers. However, it
is more likely that some consumers would prefer to pay a lower price

for a lower level of quality. By eliminating unlicensed practitioners from some markets, we are harming some consumers by denying them the right to engage in certain beneficial transactions, and we are harming all consumers by increasing the price of the service. While it may seem that it is important for physicians to be certified for quality, it is less obvious that this is important for insurance adjusters or real estate brokers or assistant horse trainers, all occupations licensed in New York State and perhaps others as well. Economists generally believe that most of these laws are aimed at increasing the earnings of practitioners, and there is evidence that licensing does increase earnings by about 15 percent. Moreover, these laws are favored by practitioners and they generally lobby the legislature for passage (Kleiner and Krueger, 2014).

An example in the news as I write this is Uber. Uber is a car service based on use of the internet. It enables drivers and potential passengers to quickly and easily find one another using an app. But most large cities have regulated taxicab markets. This means that taxi companies have lobbied the city council to limit the number of taxicabs and require licenses to operate a taxicab. There is generally a "taxicab commission" dominated by members of the industry. In many cities, Uber is engaged in a serious and highly public fight with these commissions. Of course, the commissions claim that they are "protecting" consumers from unsafe drivers, but the nature of Uber makes the falsity of this claim obvious. The only protection that is occurring is protection of existing taxicab licenses. Recently the City of New York has placed a ban on new Uber and Lyft drivers, at the behest of the taxicab industry.

Here is an example of the disadvantage of the use of the term "competition." Practitioners trying to limit others from their business (say, dentists trying to keep others from engaging in tooth whitening, a real issue that has gone to the Supreme Court) will talk about eliminating competition from incompetent practitioners. But if we thought of the issue as limiting the ability of consumers to cooperate with suppliers of their choice, the special interests might have less power.

Marketing

Economics stresses the competition between firms. However, the discipline of marketing stresses the cooperation between buyers and sellers. A leading marketing textbook, Philip Kotler and Gary Armstrong's *Principles of Marketing,* defines marketing as "defining profitable customer relationships." Chapter titles in the text include "Creating and Capturing Customer Value," "Partnering to Build Customer Relationships," and "Creating Value for Target Customers." These titles and the text itself stress the cooperative relationship between sellers and buyers. To the extent that the economy is based more on cooperation than on competition, then marketing may have done a better job of describing the economy than has economics.

Webs of Cooperation

Each transaction also involves, directly or indirectly, millions of individuals. We will never meet most of these individuals, but we still indirectly cooperate with them. Consider what appears to be a simple transaction: I use a credit card to buy a Coke from a vending machine. A little thought leads us to understand that huge numbers of people, living and dead, are involved in that transaction. To start, we may divide the transaction into three components: the Coke, the credit card, the vending machine. The Coke is itself made from a secret formula, so I don't know what is in it. But there are agricultural products, including (if it is not a Diet Coke) sugar. The sugar is grown on a farm. Growing and harvesting the sugar takes some number of people, but also some complex machines such as tractors. These machines were made using other machines which were themselves made by still other machines, many of them produced by people now dead. If we just trace the machines used in growing the sugar and other agricultural inputs for the Coke, we already have a very large number of people involved. There is also fertilizer and pesticides used in growing the sugar; each of these is the product of a large industry and millions of people directly or indirectly. The inputs must be transported to the Coke factory and the product must be transported to the location of the vending machine. This involves trucks (again, the result of complex manufacturing processes) and roads, built using complex road building machinery and financed by taxation collected by governments. The vending machine itself is a complex machine, again using many parts. The plastic bottle or aluminum can holding the Coke is an output of another hugely complex manufacturing process involving mining machinery (if a can) or petroleum drilling (if a bottle).

Now think about the credit card used to pay for the transaction. Credit cards involve at least two banks (my bank, issuing the card, and the vendor's bank, receiving the payment) and some intermediate processing agents. Each of these is a large organization, with thousands of employees. Of course, all these employees (and all the other people involved in the transaction) must eat, again involving farmers, grocery stores, trucks, more credit cards, and more people. They also consume myriad other products: clothing, shelter, books, movies, and so on. Some of them may even have learned something about their business from one of my economics courses at Emory.

These are just a few of the direct links in the transaction. Consider the background—what is called the infrastructure. The whole system runs on electricity, a huge industry itself. These days, every link in the system is connected to a computer. The vendor was willing to place the vending machine because it is fairly confident that it will not be stolen or robbed, the result of the police, which are in turn part of the government. Indeed, once we count everyone directly or indirectly involved in the transaction, it is not implausible that every employed person in the country (and many in other countries) is directly or indirectly involved in every transaction.

The point is that all these millions of people involved in the Coke transaction (and indeed, in every transaction) are cooperating with one another. The cooperation is totally impersonal and uncoordinated. Almost none of these people know one another, and many of them are dead. Moreover, some people not yet born will cooperate with these same people by using some of the same inputs. Nonetheless, the market creates a huge web of cooperation. The capitalist market economy is far and away the greatest engine for cooperation that has ever existed. Economists are fond of pointing out that this great system works with no central direction, and given its complexity it could not be centrally directed (see Soviet Union). But we economists sometimes lose sight of the fact that the entire enterprise is cooperative. Again, we must realize that competition is important; the reason the entire system of cooperation works so well is because of competition. But the competition that exists is competition for the right to cooperate, and the benefits arise from cooperation.

Note that this massive web of production and consumption is run cooperatively. Each person does what he or she wants, given prices and opportunities. We take the job we want, given opportunities. We consume the products we want. There is no coercion anywhere in the system. It is odd that today many people favor socialism, a system where the government controls what each person does and what they consume.

Complex Coordination

There is another way of viewing cooperation in markets. Individual transactions are examples of cooperation. However, many or even all events are actually the result of many individual transactions. Consider, for example, a complex meal. The meal is made of many components: bread, salad, meat, vegetables, wine, dessert, coffee. Each of these components (and subcomponents, such as salad dressing, butter, sugar, cream) was purchased. The cook, whoever he or she might be, had to purchase all these components and coordinate their preparation. But this is a simple task compared to a market.

Continuing with our meal example, consider the supermarket where the food was bought. The manager must purchase at wholesale the components. Moreover, he or she faces uncertainty in that demand on a given day might be greater or smaller than anticipated. If greater, and some item sells out, then there is an opportunity loss (the manager could have made more money if he or she had purchased more) and perhaps a loss of future business as dissatisfied customers shop elsewhere. If demand is smaller and the item is perishable, then there are losses from spoilage. We can trace similar decisions up the food chain, to the wholesaler, the packager, and the farmer. At each step, there are markets mediated by price, and decisions must be made. What is truly remarkable about a market economy is that all these decisions are coordinated through cooperative market transactions. At the end of the day, the grocery store ends up with approximately the mix of foods that the customers desire, and the restaurant ends up selling completed meals to hungry diners. Moreover, similar chains of coordinated transactions occur throughout the economy.

Terms of Transactions

Because transactions are cooperative, buyers and sellers have many interests in common in structuring a transaction. Indeed, except for one term, buyers and sellers want the identical transaction. The transaction they want is what economists call the most efficient transaction, the one that maximizes the joint gains between the two parties. The only term they disagree about is the price term, which decides how the buyers and sellers will divide the gains. Buyers, of course, want a low price so that they can get more of the gains, and sellers want a higher price for the same reason. But except for price, parties will ultimately agree on the other terms.

This agreement may not be obvious. It might appear that each party would prefer terms that provided more benefits to itself. But a little thought shows that this is not so. Assume, for example, that buyers want a more durable product, which will cost an extra five dollars to produce. It might seem that sellers would prefer to save the five dollars and make a shoddy product. But assume that buyers are willing to pay six dollars for the extra durability. Then it is in the interest of sellers to produce the higher-quality product because they can make more money by producing it. As long as they can sell the higher-quality product for an extra $5.01 or more, they gain by making it. If buyers can buy it for $5.99 or less, they will buy it. The parties may disagree on the additional price for the more durable version, but if it is between $5.01 and $5.99, both parties have an interest in the more durable product being produced and sold.

Here is one of the roles of competition. Buyers would prefer to pay a low price, but sellers want a high price. However, if there is sufficient competition among sellers, the price will be forced down to the lowest possible level. Conversely, if the product is in short supply, then competition among buyers will force the price up. This higher price will, of course, create an incentive for sellers to produce more so that in the next period the product will not be in such short supply. This is what I meant when I said that competition has an important role in setting the terms of cooperation. The transaction is cooperative, but the terms are set by competition. Moreover, if another seller should appear who can sell at a lower price, that seller will get the business. Competition not only determines the terms of the transaction, it also determines which parties will engage in the transaction. But the transaction itself is cooperative.

Competition also provides information: What is the lowest cost? Who should produce the product? Should more or less be produced? All this information is generated by the cooperative market system. Moreover, remarkably, virtually all the information someone needs to participate in the system is conveyed by price. I need not know what has generated the increase in price of coffee; if I observe it, that is a signal to me to consume less of it. This economy of information is one of the important factors making the functioning of markets possible. It also shows why socialism, where price is divorced from costs, does not work.

Take a more complex term. Assume that Contractor is building a house for Buyer and that there is some danger that the house might burn down before it is finished. Who should bear this risk? Again, the first thought might be that each party would want the other to bear the risk. But think about the actual economics of the issue. For Contractor to prevent a fire, he or she need only take some simple precautions: At the end of the day, make sure all fires are out and perhaps that all electrical equipment is unplugged. Since Contractor and his workers are on the job site anyway, these precautions will be inexpensive, perhaps on the order of an extra $500 for a house. On the other hand, if Buyer must drive by the building site every day until the house is finished and do the inspection himself, this will be time-consuming and much more expensive, perhaps on the order of $1,000. Then both parties have an interest in Contractor bearing the risk. Again, Buyer might want to pay only $500 for Contractor to bear the risk, and Contractor might want to charge $1,000, but both parties agree that Contractor should bear the risk and undertake the effort to prevent fires. They agree on the terms of inspection. Put another way, Buyer would be willing to pay up to $1,000 more for a house that he or she need not inspect daily, and Contractor would be willing to accept $500 to undertake the inspection. Given this, there is clearly room for a deal whereby Contractor accepts the risk of the house burning down and spends the effort to avoid this outcome, and Buyer pays Contractor for bearing this risk.

This example brings up another point. In many cases there will be no explicit bargaining over price or other terms. Rather, if there are many buyers and sellers in the market—what I have been calling a perfectly cooperative market and what is normally called a perfectly competitive market—then price and other terms will be determined by the market. In the Contractor-Buyer example, it will be standard for Contractors to accept liability for such fires, and prices for houses as quoted will always assume that this is the pattern. Because of this relationship in a modern economy, buyers and sellers will seldom if ever actually bargain over prices for standardized goods. Prices will be set in a market, as will other terms. Again, competition sets the terms for cooperation.

If there is negotiation over terms in an exchange, it may appear that the parties are disagreeing such that there is conflict rather than cooperation. There are two reasons for this apparent disagreement. First, there is simple disagreement about price. Buyer wants a low price, Seller a high price. Each party has an incentive to keep true preferences about the reservation price (the maximum price Buyer is willing to pay or the minimum price Seller is willing to accept) secret because that will enable the party to increase its own gains from the transaction. That is, if Buyer knows that Seller is willing to sell for five dollars, then buyer will not pay any more than this. But if Buyer does not know Seller's reservation price (the lowest price at which Seller will sell), then Buyer may be induced to pay more than five dollars. Similarly, if Seller knows Buyer's true reservation price, he can get a higher price for his goods. Thus, much negotiation in contracts is about price, with each party trying to maximize its own gains. Sometimes there will be no agreement and the parties will walk away. This may be either because there was no mutually agreeable price (higher quality costs five dollars to produce so Seller will not sell for less than this, but it is only worth $4.50 to Buyer), or it may be because the parties bargained too hard and were unable to discover a mutually agreeable price. In complex transactions, "price" may include terms and timing of payment and other details.

A second reason for bargaining in contractual negotiations is that the parties may not know who can best (most cheaply) perform some function. Is it less costly for Buyer or Seller to inspect the goods? Can Buyer more easily paint the goods, or is it cheaper to include painting in the production process? Who can most cheaply add custom features to the goods? During the bargaining process, the parties will negotiate over these issues, with the negotiation taking the form of offers and acceptances: "I'll pay three dollars more if you paint the widget." "No, I want four dollars." An agreement will be reached, and the agreement will lead to each party performing that part of the contract which it can do most cheaply, but negotiation will be involved to make this determination. Information is costly, and the negotiation process may be a way of gathering useful information. But the existence of negotiation should not blind us to the fact that, if the deal is eventually done, both parties will gain, and the ultimate agreement will create joint gains and will be an example of cooperation.

Moreover, for many exchanges, there will be no negotiation. For many contracts, competition will set the terms so closely that there is no room for negotiation. For example, as mentioned above, Contractors will always be liable for a property burning down during construction. Many consumer contracts are of this form. Consumers often cannot bargain over the terms of contracts. Lawyers sometimes misunderstand this and assume that consumers have no bargaining power and are helpless victims. But it is more likely that the terms are set by competition in the marketplace, and there is no negotiation because the terms are as favorable as can be. Negotiation over the terms of a contract is actually an indication that the market is not what is normally called perfectly competitive (or what I call perfectly cooperative). Negotiation is a sign of some market imperfection—often a small number of buyers and sellers. In a market with many buyers and sellers—a perfectly competitive (cooperative) market—there is no negotiation.

Networks and Platforms

Network effects are a nice example of cooperation in a marketplace. Network effects are said to exist when the value of some good or service increases as more people use that good or service. Email or texting are recent examples: If only a few people use these methods of communication, they are not very useful. But as more people use the services, their value increases because each person can communicate with more users. Though the users are not consciously setting out to cooperate with one another, in fact the network creates a web of cooperation. Product developers often understand this and consciously seek more users (more cooperators) to increase the value of their product. Current examples are Twitter, Facebook, and LinkedIn, all of which exist because of network effects. Indeed, these exist solely as networks. Without the network of other users, these products would be worthless. If you look at the Android or Apple app stores, you will find numerous new entrants trying to become the creators of the next network app.

In the case of the Apple products, there was an additional source of network effects. The iPhone is compatible with regular phone, email, and texting services and so did not create a network effect itself. However, important components of these products are the ancillary goods and services associated with them. The most important are the apps that greatly increase the utility of the products. By being first, Apple could develop a large community of app creators who specialized in the Apple operating system. There were other ancillary products associated with iPhones and tablets: for example, chargers, keyboards, cases, and speakers. These were examples of firms cooperating with Apple to create a more valuable set of products and thus increase cooperation with consumers.

Moreover, much of Apple's profits come from advertising. By creating a network, Apple could increase consumer use of its products and therefore increase the value of its advertising on those products. Advertising is itself a highly cooperative endeavor with numerous parts. There is the platform that displays the ad. There is the advertiser who pays for the ad. There is the consumer who sees the ad and acts on it. There is the advertising agency that places the ad. In modern advertising, there are many additional firms involved with various parts of the business. These pieces cooperate through the market to provide advertising and to inform consumers about opportunities for consumption.

A particular and important generalization of a network is a "platform." A platform is something that brings together a network of buyers and a network of sellers. The major platforms today are Apple, Google, Amazon, eBay, and Facebook. In these cases, buyers and sellers use the platform to find one another in order to engage in cooperative acts. For example, on Google, sellers bid instantaneously for the right to show ads to consumers who have engaged in certain searches. Thus, consumers come to Google to find goods to buy, and sellers try to find these buyers. Similarly, Amazon, in addition to selling products itself, also sells products of other sellers. These platforms are actively competing with one another for the right to cooperate with buyers and sellers. Moreover, each of these firms is continually adding services and improving performance so as to increase the value and usage of its network.

The existence of networks also illustrates the benefit of competition. Because several networks are competing with one another for the right to cooperate with consumers, costs and prices to consumers are kept to the lowest feasible level. For example, when Apple created the first mobile phone, Google (now Alphabet) created the Android network to compete, even to the point of giving away the technology to anyone who wanted to create an Android product. Otherwise, Apple would have had a monopoly, which would have harmed both Google and consumers.

Bad Transactions

So far, I have argued that transactions are mutually beneficial and cooperative. But today many readers may have a different impression. It may appear that most transactions are one-sided or that consumers lose from most transactions. There are "consumer reporters" on the nightly news and in many newspapers who find consumers who have been harmed in some transaction and publicize that transaction and the associated harm. There are many government agencies (my old agencies, the Federal Trade Commission and the Consumer Product Safety Commission, and others, such as the Securities and Exchange Commission, the Food and Drug Administration, and the new Consumer Financial Protection Bureau) which specialize in "protecting" consumers from harmful transactions. There are books by Ralph Nader and his intellectual descendants that warn about the dangers of the marketplace. There are product liability and other lawsuits about harmful transactions.

But for all this, almost all transactions almost all the time work well with no need for government or any other intervention. Consumer reporters have stories to report exactly because most transactions work and the ones that do not are newsworthy. Consider the financial crisis of 2008. News stories would indicate that most mortgages defaulted, leading to a crisis. In fact, of about fifty million mortgages in the U.S., in 2011 only about eight hundred thousand were in default. This created a serious problem, but my point is that most mortgage transactions, even in a time of crisis, were sound.

Consider yourself as a consumer. You buy thousands of products each year: food items in a grocery store, health and beauty aids in a drugstore, meals in restaurants, clothing in department or specialty stores, electronic goods from Best Buy or Amazon, an automobile and gasoline, phone service, medical care, and many other things. You are satisfied with the results of almost all these transactions. (Of course, you wish that everything were cheaper, but we agree that buyers and sellers will disagree on the price term of a transaction.) Sometimes a transaction will go bad: A restaurant meal may be cold or overcooked, some meat or produce from a grocery store may be spoiled, a shirt may shrink when washed, your phone will drop too many calls, or it may catch fire during the charging process. Something you have purchased in the past may be recalled. You may remember these bad transactions and complain about the shoddy quality of today's products. But even in these cases, almost all merchants will refund your money or give you another product. Even if you remember the bad experiences and forget the good ones (like a consumer reporter or a government regulatory agency), some thought indicates that the overwhelming majority of transactions are mutually beneficial.

Moreover, these transactions are beneficial because it is in the interest of both parties to make them beneficial. It might appear that the government agencies mentioned above are the main forces policing transactions and that without them the marketplace would be rife with fraud and deception. However, this is not so. Market forces alone guarantee that most transactions will be beneficial. Reputation is the main driver of this feature of transactions.

First, consider consumers as buyers. Nowadays, many transactions are through credit cards. In the past, many consumers had access to other forms of credit. Our largest purchases—houses, cars, college educations—are often financed through long-term loans. It might appear that consumer-borrowers could save money by simply defaulting on some of these loans. But of course, we know that if we do so, our credit rating—our reputation as a reliable borrower—will be destroyed. This reputation is very valuable: For example, it can mean lower borrowing costs next time we buy a house or even the ability to borrow at all. Thus, even though we could cheat on a transaction, it does not generally pay to do so. It pays to maintain our reputation.

The same forces operate even more strongly on the other side of the market as well. The seller's reputation is very important. In the past, when markets were local, word of mouth among acquaintances would provide information about the honesty and reliability of sellers. In some markets that method still operates. For example, an important study of the diamond market in New York has shown that local reputation effects can still be important (Bernstein, 1992).

As the market began to expand—that is, as webs of cooperation became larger—other methods of guaranteeing reputation came into being. Institutions such as the Better Business Bureau and *Consumer Reports* magazine were aimed at conveying this information to consumers. This is where consumer reporters in newspapers and on TV have a useful function.

It also pays for sellers themselves to establish reputations. When markets were local, this was easy to do. Consumers would shop in local stores and would quickly learn if merchants were honest. As markets expanded—as webs of cooperation grew larger—it became more difficult to directly create reputations. One mechanism was brand names. If a seller invests in a brand name, perhaps by advertising, then this investment becomes a bond. If the seller cheats, say, by offering lower quality than promised, then this reputation capital is lost. National retailers (Sears, J. C. Penney, A&P) performed this function for retailing. Similarly, product brand names (GE, Coca-Cola) guaranteed product quality across the national marketplace. Trademark law, which protects the brand name and allows firms whose trademark is stolen to sue for damages, provided a private mechanism for enforcing these reputation-enhancing methods.

Another interesting institution was franchising. As many markets became more national (due in part to the interstate highway system), it became valuable for traveling consumers to be able to learn about quality in different locations. This was exactly the function of franchised outlets. A consumer visiting Ohio who knew McDonald's from

California could be relatively sure of obtaining the same menu and quality in Ohio as he or she was used to in California. In part, this was the function of the franchisor: McDonald's would ensure quality by inspecting franchised outlets and enforcing quality standards.

Now, the internet provides additional methods of verifying reputation. For example, eBay provides information of seller reliability. Amazon and other websites provide consumer comments, which are another important source for information about quality and other seller and product characteristics. Providing such information is the business plan of Yelp.

Cooperation through Contract

A contract is the legal document, enforceable by a court, which governs relationships between parties. Contracts are the legal basis for cooperation. The simplest function of a contract is to facilitate exchange, and an exchange is a cooperative relationship. Many exchanges are nonsimultaneous (I may pay in advance for a house that you promise to build for me, or you may build the house because I have promised to pay you when it is finished), and contracts make such exchanges possible. In this sense, a legal system that enforces contracts is important to increase the level of cooperation which is possible in an economy. Even though a transaction is cooperative and mutually beneficial, in many exchanges it might be possible for one person to break the agreement and gain even more. The gains from breaking some contract may be greater than the loss in reputation which the breach will create. Thus, the purpose of legally enforceable contracts is to limit this ability. That is, a legally enforceable contract will limit the ability of a party to gain by cheating on the contract. But because each party knows this, legal enforceability of contracts increases the scope for cooperation by increasing the willingness of parties to enter into exchanges that they otherwise would be afraid to undertake.

A contract governs exchanges which occur over time. However, at any given time, one party or the other might have an incentive to cheat. I ship you goods and you have promised to pay, but when you have the goods and have not yet paid, you have an incentive not to pay. Or you pay in advance, and I have an incentive not to ship the goods. Emory has paid me for next month, and I have not yet taught my courses. Almost all contracts will create instances where it would appear to pay for one party or the other to break the contract. However, when the parties write the contract, both know this, and so both have incentives to commit themselves not to break the contract in this or other ways. Therefore, even though contracts are cooperative, we may see what appear to be harsh terms to penalize a party who beaks the contract. It may seem that the other party has imposed these terms, but it will often be in my interest to write a contract penalizing me if I break the contract to induce you to do business with me. In other words, the fact that some contracts have harsh terms for breach by no means says that contracts are not cooperative. In writing a contract, parties cooperate on deciding who will do which task and in deciding what the penalties will be if one party breaks the contract.

The study of law may bias one against the cooperative view of contracts. This is because legal cases studied in law schools involve contracts that did not work. That is, the study of contract law is the study of failed contracts. Even reading about contracts in the news may create such a bias because news stories are only generated when there is a conflict. Contracts that work are not newsworthy. ("Millions of workers cheerfully went to work today because they were satisfied with the terms of their compensation" is not a story; a strike is a story. But strikes are rare.) However, most contracts do not fail; most work. Most contracts are not litigated. These do not get studied in law schools and are not in casebooks since there is no case, and they are not reported in the news. Some lawyers specialize in transactions, and these lawyers write the contracts that actually run businesses. But their work is less studied in law schools. Nonetheless, studying failed contracts enables practitioners to draft contracts that are less likely to fail because through studying failed deals, practitioners learn about ways to avoid failure. But it is important to keep in mind that these failures are the exception, not the rule.

There is another reason why those trained in law may miss the cooperative nature of exchange. In a large transaction between businesses or between firms and unions, lawyers will write the contracts. The parties will bargain over terms, either to find the best price or to find out who can best perform each part of the deal. But the lawyer is involved in writing the contract because of the bargaining of the parties. In most consumer contracts, there is no such bargaining. One party—generally, the seller—writes the contract, and the buyer is in a "take it or leave it" position. Lawyers and law school professors, observing the situation, may believe that the consumer is disadvantaged by the lack of bargaining. In fact, the consumer is protected by the market, which provides more protection than would actual bargaining, but because this protection is invisible, lawyers may miss it.

Some cooperative arrangements can be sustained without contracts. Economists call these "self-enforcing agreements." A paradigm example is the sale of goods between businesses. Each period, I send you some cloth which you then make into shirts, and then you sell the shirts. I send you the cloth each month, and you pay me. If you don't pay me one month, then I simply stop sending you the cloth. You have an incentive to pay because the present value of the future business is worth more than the one-month payment you can gain by cheating. Businesspeople often say they have a "deal" rather than a contract, referring to this sort of arrangement. Much of business runs on this type of agreement, without reliance on formal written contracts (Telser, 1990).

Reputations can also sustain cooperation. If I have a reputation for honoring my agreements, then this is a valuable asset. If I cheat you and others learn about it, then I have lost the value of this asset. This creates a strong incentive for me to not cheat. There are also formal mechanisms for providing information about reputation. For example, the Better Business Bureau will certify companies. More importantly today, firms like eBay report percentage of "positive feed-back" for sellers, thus certifying the seller's reputation. Amazon often sells products for other firms, thus using Amazon's reputation to guar-antee other sellers. In general, the internet has been very useful in certifying reputations and so increasing possibilities of cooperation. But it is important to remember that markets were fundamentally cooperative before the internet.

Franchising: An Example

Modern business is extremely complex, and much of that complex-ity is governed by contract. For an example, consider franchising. Some firm (McDonald's, for example) has discovered a business plan involving rapid selling of highly standardized and quality-controlled hamburgers and french fries, and the store is making a lot of money. The owner realizes that there is a chance to make much more money by opening more stores. Moreover, these stores would benefit by using the same name as the original because this would provide consumers information about the product for sale. However, there is a problem: For the business to work, there must be an on-site local manager with a strong incentive to work hard in monitoring the quality of the prod-uct. A salary for the manager would not provide sufficient incentives. So there are two parts to the business: a business plan and local moni-toring. The solution to combining these two parts is the cooperative business plan called franchising, where the franchisor (McDonald's) provides the business plan and brand name, and the local owner (the franchisee) provides the local management and monitoring.

The arrangement is still not complete. Other terms are needed. Each store benefits by being part of a franchise chain because when consumers see a McDonald's sign, they know what to expect. But there is a chance for free riding: if one store degrades the product (perhaps by slow service, perhaps by low quality, such as stale buns), that store will bear some cost because it will lose some repeat business. But all McDonald's stores will lose as well because the reputation of the brand has been depreciated. The franchisor also will lose because the value of the brand has been reduced, so he or she will not be able to charge as much for future franchises. Thus, the individual store reaps the entire saving from poor service and bears only a fraction of the cost. This would create an incentive for excessive shirking, and the value of the brand would quickly fall to zero as more and more franchisees begin to cheat. This creates an incentive for the franchisor to monitor the quality of each of the stores. But for the monitoring to be effective, the franchisor must have some power to enforce its quality standards. This means that the franchise contract will enable the franchisor to terminate a franchise relatively easily.

More recently, many businesses have replaced the franchise relationship with a contractual alternative, the "managing partner," who has a partial ownership in the local business, which creates incentives for monitoring similar to those of a franchisee. (This institution has grown because many states, prodded by local franchisees who are voters in the state, have passed laws interfering with the terms of the franchise contract and making it more difficult to terminate underperforming franchisees.)

Franchising is just one example of complex cooperation through contract. If we look deeply into any modern business, we will find highly complex patterns of cooperation governed by contract. Consider a smartphone, a product that many of us know and love. The product is made by one company (say, Samsung) using software made by another (Android, by Google) and made of components made by other companies, and perhaps assembled by still another company. The product is then operated by another company, perhaps Verizon, which cooperates contractually with Samsung for the terms on which the phone will be sold and used. The phone is valuable because of the apps, made by still other companies. All these interactions are cooperative, and all are governed by complex contracts. Indeed, even the relationship between the consumer and the carrier is complex and itself is governed by a complex contract which the carrier makes available (and which no rational consumer will read or has ever read).

I recently attended a seminar on fracking (oil and natural gas mining through "fracturing" the rock containing the deposits) and learned that a modern oil well is a highly cooperative endeavor involving several companies manufacturing drill bits, pipes, and other capital equipment; producers of drilling equipment; producers of chemicals; the owner of the well; and many other parties. Once the oil or natural gas is available, it will be shipped through pipelines or by railroad, owned by various cooperating companies, refined by other businesses, and sold by still others. Again, these relationships are cooperative, not competitive, and are governed by complex contracts.

Labor Contracts

Labor is classically called one of the "factors of production": land, labor, and capital. These factors are employed by an entrepreneur who then creates a business. Economists sometimes write a mathematical equation relating these inputs, called a "production function." But what this equation represents is the cooperation between the factors and entrepreneur in producing output.

Unlike land or capital, workers have their own utility functions and sets of goals and desires. For example, workers might want to "shirk," to not work as hard as they promised. The amount of money a worker makes is a function of how hard he or she works. If the worker works harder, then the worker produces more and is worth more to the firm. If the worker shirks, the worker is worth less. Both labor (workers) and managers know that shirking is a potential problem. Therefore, the wage paid to a worker will depend on the expected amount of shirking. This creates an incentive for a cooperative arrangement between workers and managers to reduce the amount of shirking. That is, if workers and managers can agree on some method of reducing shirking by workers, both can benefit and wages for workers can be higher.

This is an important point. One might think that employers have incentives to make workers work hard, and workers have incentives not to work so hard. But workers know that they will be paid based on how hard they are expected to work, and so they have incentives to accept contractual terms that provide incentives for them to work hard. This means that contracts with proper incentives are cooperatively agreed upon by both workers and managers. Indeed, managers are themselves employees of the firm, and they will also be governed by mutually agreed incentive contracts. The nature of the contract depends on the tasks of the worker. A production worker may be paid for output: a piece-rate contract, creating an incentive to produce more. A salesperson may be paid commission, creating an incentive to sell more. The manager may be paid based on the profitability of the division, creating an incentive to properly balance costs and revenues. The CEO and other top executives may be paid in stock options or other terms determined by the value of the firm itself. This creates an incentive to balance capital and output across divisions of the firm. In these cases, it might at first appear that the contract is biased in favor of the firm and against the employee, but in fact all of them are mutually beneficial because they create incentives for optimal effort by the worker and so increase the payment received by the worker. All of them are deeply cooperative.

There is one exception to the efficiency argument. To an employer, a worker is an input like any other, but to the worker, the job is very important. Moreover, since at any given time workers have what they view as the best job, losing that job will create a loss in utility, even if another is found quickly. Therefore, workers place a greater value on maintaining employment than would be efficient from the perspective of the employer.

Employers have three options given this preference of workers. They can ignore workers' preferences. However, this will lead to dissatisfied and probably inferior workers, so it is not an option for jobs that require dedication and commitment. Employers can continue to hire and fire workers as needed but pay workers a higher salary to compensate for the uncertainty this policy creates. Finally, employers can implicitly or even explicitly (through contract) agree to provide some job security even if the employee is not needed at some point in time. The extreme example is in my business, academia, where tenure contracts mean that many professors are retained long after their productivity has greatly decreased. The existence of this form of job protection means that on average universities can pay lower salaries than otherwise because of the associated job security. However, it also means that on average professors will be more risk averse than otherwise because the business attracts employees who place a high value on job security.

Government indirectly interferes in this process. Since the 1930s, the U.S. government has encouraged labor unions, and labor unions make it excessively difficult to eliminate workers, by processes such as seniority. Some unions also seek work rules which lead to excessive usage of labor, called "featherbedding." As a result, union shops are less efficient than other workplaces. Perhaps because of this, the percentage of union workers in the private sector has been declining in recent years. It could be that employers are able to offer sufficient wage premiums so that workers are willing to forgo the benefits of extra job security and other benefits provided by a union.

One exception is the public sector, where unionization has been growing. Interestingly enough, in many jurisdictions, employers have no preference for efficiency. Union members are also citizens, and in many jurisdictions they will vote for politicians who support inefficient hiring. Moreover, in these jurisdictions, union dues can be donated as political contributions to politicians who support additional hiring. Michael Bloomberg, the former mayor of New York City (which is greatly subject to these pressures from public sector unions) has called this the "labor-electoral complex." This is a form of cooperation which does not serve the public interest. It is essentially cooperation between public sector workers and politicians to rip off voter-taxpayers. The limit is Detroit, which has gone bankrupt.

A recent Supreme Court case, *Janus v. American Federation of State, County, and Municipal Employees Council 31*, 2018, has greatly weakened the power of public unions. Workers can no longer be forced to join unions and pay union dues. Since union dues are used in part for political contributions, this case will also have important political implications.

In addition to cooperation in producing output, workers and firms also cooperate in training, in creating what economists call "human capital." Nobel Prize laureate Gary Becker (1964) discussed two forms of human capital: "general" human capital and "specific" human capital. General capital is useful in a wide variety of businesses. It is the sort of training supplied by schools: general literacy, math skills, and more advanced training in universities and graduate schools. Employers will in general not pay for acquisition of general human capital because there is no way they can recover the cost of such training. A worker is made more productive, but the productivity is available to any employer, and so the full value will go to the worker. If the worker acquires general human capital on the job, the worker himself will pay for this training by accepting a lower wage during the training period. This is part of the reason why entry-level jobs pay low salaries—they often contain significant training. Even after completing schooling, the worker needs general business skills, and firms provide these in return for a lower wage—in the case of interns, sometimes a zero wage.

Specific human capital is valuable only to the firm. Some examples are knowledge of the firm's accounting practices, production techniques, and of the particular organizational structure of the firm. Acquisition of this form of capital makes the worker more productive and so more valuable to the particular firm, but not to other firms. Thus, workers and firms will jointly pay for this capital (workers by accepting a reduced wage in return for the training, firms by providing the training), and the returns will be divided between the workers and the firms.

There is another twist to general human capital. In most cases, workers pay for acquisition of general human capital by accepting lower wages. However, there are some forms of general human capital that workers cannot pay for because the human capital is too valuable. An example would be a valuable trade secret in a production method. Here the value of the asset (say, Coca-Cola's secret formula) would be so great that the worker could work for free and still not pay for the value. One way to induce firms to provide this training is to make it specific by forbidding the worker from taking the skills elsewhere. This can be done through a "covenant not to compete," a contractual term that forbids the worker from using this training at another firm. In order to induce a worker to accept such a contract, the employer must pay an above-market wage. However, the employer can pay such a wage because the worker is worth more to this firm than to others, exactly because of the possession of what has become specific human capital.

Capital

Owners of capital make their capital available to those who can productively employ it and in turn are compensated for making the capital available. Payments for capital may be in the form of interest or dividends. As modern economies have become more complex, so the forms of capital have also become more complex, and students of finance study many potential capital instruments governed by a large number of contracts. The ultimate purpose of these contracts is to facilitate cooperation between those who have capital to lend and those who can productively use that capital.

The contracts between owners and users of capital may be very complex. Lawyers sometimes view contracts in terms of bargaining power and assume that the party with the greatest bargaining power will dictate the terms of the contract. But this is incorrect. In general, both parties want essentially the same terms for the contract (again excepting price).

Consider a supplier of capital to a firm: a lender or an investor. The lender wants to be sure that the loan will be repaid. To protect this capital, the lender may insist on certain terms in the contract. For example, the lender may want liens on some of the equipment of the firm so that he or she can repossess this equipment if the borrower does not pay back the loan, perhaps with a severe penalty for default. The borrower might agree to these terms. If so, it might appear that the contract is one-sided in favor of the lender. A lawyer might say that the lender had more bargaining power.

But in fact, the borrower might have just as much interest in these terms as the lender. Remember that the price term is one on which the parties may disagree. The price of borrowing is the interest rate. If a loan is riskier, then the interest rate paid by the borrower will be higher. But if the penalty for default is higher, then the borrower has a stronger incentive not to default, and since the lender is more likely to get his money back, the interest rate can be lower. Both parties know this. If default is less likely, then the interest rate charged will be lower. Thus, the borrower will have a strong incentive to commit to repayment and will be willing to sign a contract creating such incentives to lower his borrowing costs. Thus, these contracts are cooperative.

There are several issues between borrowers and lenders. Most of these are studied by economists under the term "agency costs."

An agency cost exists when the incentives of the "principal" and the "agent" are not perfectly aligned. In the case of a firm, the stockholders are the principals, and the employees of the firm, including the managers, are the agents. Ideally, the agents would perfectly represent the interest of the principals, but it is difficult to perfectly align incentives. Contracts between principals and agents set the terms of cooperation, and both parties want these terms to be as efficient as possible because efficient contracts create a larger surplus for both parties to divide.

Here is one example. Think of an entrepreneur who has started a firm and owns it now. For various reasons he or she may want to sell part of the firm to make it into a publicly held corporation. The entrepreneur may want to expand and need more money, or may simply want to diversify the investment for safety, or he or she may want to "cash out" and use some of the value for consumption. In any case, the entrepreneur will sell stock, and the firm will become a corporation. But in so doing, the entrepreneur will increase the number of people with whom he or she is cooperating and will be forced to give up some control. In particular, there will now be a board of directors supervising the behavior of the firm and of the former owner, who is now a manager.

Continue the example. Suppose the manager (who may have been the entrepreneur or may be a newly hired manager) undertakes a risky investment. Say there is a 25 percent chance that the value of the firm will double and a 75 percent chance that the investment will not pay and the firm will go bankrupt. This might be a good deal from the viewpoint of the manager if he or she now owns no stock and is a salaried employee. If the investment pays off, then the individual is running twice as large a firm. If it does not, then he or she will simply find another job, although the person's pay may be lower because a firm he or she directed has failed. From the viewpoint of the owners, the deal is bad because the expected value of the bet is negative. So the owners want to put in place a contract that will discourage this sort of investment. The simplest method is the board of directors. The board has oversight of the firm, representing the stockholders' interests, and can approve or disapprove major decisions, such as those that put the firm itself at risk.

Notice that both the entrepreneur selling shares in his firm and the investors buying shares have an interest in creating this board. The investors want it to protect their investment. The entrepreneur wants a board because he or she can sell stock on much more favorable terms if investors know they have control and that risk-taking will be limited. Thus, although it might appear that the board represents the interests of the investors, in fact both parties agree that this mechanism is valuable. It increases the value of the company, and so both parties gain. Again, a cooperative agreement.

There are many other mechanisms with the same properties. This is not a book on agency theory or on corporate finance, so I am not going to elaborate on all these mechanisms. But the point is that they are all cooperative and that both parties agree on the terms of these agreements because they serve to increase the value of the company (Rubin, 1990).

Specialization

An important source of gains from cooperation and trade is specialization and its twin, "division of labor." Specialization is the essence of cooperation: I do one task, you do another, and we cooperatively produce some final output. Or I produce one thing, you produce another, and we cooperatively trade so we each have some of each good.

Specialization is so essential to our nature as humans that it is hard to conceive of a world without it, except for Robinson Crusoe before Friday or Tom Hanks in *Cast Away*, and anyway both these fictional characters had access to some cooperatively produced artifacts from the crashed boat or plane. All known real humans engage in some specialization. In hunter-gatherer societies, there is specialization by gender and age. Men generally specialize in hunting and women in gathering. Young males often specialize in war, either defensive or offensive. Older men may teach younger men how to hunt or fight. Females specialize in child care and food gathering and preparation. There may be relatively little additional specialization in such societies, but there is some.

The essence of specialization is cooperation through trade. In a modern economy, no one is self-sufficient. Indeed, no one can make anything. Production of even the simplest product is the result of massive amounts of trade and exchange. A famous essay indicates that "No One Can Make a Pencil" (Read, 1958).

Specialization occurs when one task is subdivided into several parts and individuals begin to undertake a subset of these tasks, or when new tasks are added. This is only possible if there is trade in the economy. I don't need to grow my own food or sew my own clothes because I can trade with others who will grow food and sew clothes for me. Of course, I do not trade with them directly; my students do not come to class with chickens or shirts to trade. Rather, I sell my services to the university, which charges students for these services. Using money as a medium of exchange, we all engage in massive systems of multilateral exchange. But the basis for this exchange is specialization.

Just as we discussed coordinated and uncoordinated cooperation, so we may consider coordinated and uncoordinated specialization. Coordinated specialization takes place within a firm. The overall task of the firm—say, producing pins—is subdivided into many subtasks, and each worker specializes in one of those subtasks. This is the specialization discussed by Adam Smith in *Wealth of Nations* in his famous analysis of the pin factory. Specialization can lead to subdividing tasks so that each person can do only one particular thing. The paradigm case is still Smith's pin factory, where Smith indicated that in manufacturing pins in a factory, "One man draws out the wire, another straights it, a third cuts it, a fourth points it, a fifth grinds it at the top for receiving the head; to make the head requires two or three distinct operations; to put it on, is a peculiar business, to whiten the pins is another; it is even a trade by itself to put them into the paper; and the important business of making a pin is, in this manner, divided into about eighteen distinct operations, which, in some manufactories, are all performed by distinct hands, though in others the same man will sometimes perform two or three of them." By this specialization, output per person increased from perhaps one pin per day per person to 4,800 pins per day per person.

The market itself is the source of uncoordinated specialization. Each of us can specialize in one task because we are able to acquire all our wants in a market where the goods and services are produced by other specialists.

How much specialization will there be? The answer also goes back to Smith, who told us that "the division of labor is limited by the extent of the market." That is, as there are more and more people with whom to trade, it is possible for each person to undertake a narrower and narrower set of tasks—to become more specialized. Therefore, there was relatively little specialization in our hunter-gatherer ancestors: societies were too small to allow much specialization. For example, assume someone was a good toolmaker. He could make ten stone axes per day, but the group only could use a total of fifty stone axes, and stone axes normally lasted one year. Then the toolmaker could spend only about five days per year making axes. This person might spend a few hours per week making axes but would spend the rest of his time as an unspecialized hunter. He would have been the axe maker, but he would have been relatively unspecialized.

Once our ancestors settled down, societies became larger, and there was more scope for specialization. The process has not yet ended. As costs of transportation and trade have been falling, markets have been becoming larger, and specialization has been increasing. For an earlier example, railroads in the U.S. greatly expanded the size of markets and so created room for more specialized businesses and individuals. The advent of the steamship led to greatly increased international trade, and the technology of container shipping has led to even more dramatic reductions in international shipping costs so that many markets have become worldwide and again increased possibilities of specialization. Most workers do jobs that are extremely narrow. I frequently ask people I meet on airplanes or elsewhere about their occupation, and I find that in most cases, as they explain their jobs, I quickly become lost because they do something that is so narrow as to be incomprehensible to anyone in another industry.

Or think of my field, academic economics. In a small university, there may be only a few economists, each teaching courses in a variety of fields. As a university becomes larger, there is more room for specialization. Some people may be very good at teaching basic economics and may spend all their time doing that. Others may teach in rather narrow, more advanced areas. For example, most of my teaching is in the area of "Law and Economics," a field of economics that did not even exist when I went to graduate school but has become increasingly important as the market for economics has expanded and allowed more specialization. Other colleagues teach health economics, or micro- or macro-economic theory, or econometrics (itself divided into time series and cross section), or industrial organization, and each of these fields in turn is further subdivided. Moreover, economists also write articles published in research journals. These journals are becoming increasingly specialized as the field of economics grows. The research topics are themselves evidence of a very high degree of specialization; I have a PhD in economics, but in most field journals outside my area I have difficulty understanding the titles of many articles, let alone the articles themselves. This is a further example of increased specialization as the market (in this case, the market for economists and economics) has grown. Other successful academic fields have similar degrees of specialization.

Many of us think of the medical profession when we think of specialists and specialization. Again, this increased degree of specialization is a result of increasing market size. The old general practitioner may have practiced in a small town or in a neighborhood where there was room for only one doctor who treated a wide variety of conditions. The advent of the automobile was a major factor in increasing the size of the medical market; now patients from all over town could see the same specialist doctor. As markets grew, specialization continually increased. For example, there were eye doctors. Now there are specialists in children's conditions, glaucoma, macular degeneration, retinal surgery, cataract surgery, keratotomy, and additional areas as well. Moreover, the specialist doctors have generated many other specialists: eye doctors employ trained assistants who perform various functions during the examination and treatment. Again, all of this is due to increasing market size.

These same principles can explain the boundary between coordinated and uncoordinated specialization, or between the firm (coordinated specialization) and the market (uncoordinated specialization). The size of the firm is a race between costs of coordination in the firm and costs of using markets. At first, large mainframe computers reduced costs of internal control and so led some firms to become larger. But smaller powerful desktop and laptop computers, and even phones, have enabled more decentralization. Entities such as Craigslist and Fiverr have created the "gig economy" where people can be hired for one specialized job and so enabled some firms to become smaller. Moreover, possibilities of subcontracting (facilitated by the internet) and reduced transportation costs have even led to the creation of "virtual firms," firms with very few employees who subcontract out most of the functions that previously were done within the firm.

So far, I have been discussing specialization within a country. But there is also tremendous specialization across countries. Much of this is due to the increasing size of the market caused by reduced transportation costs and reduced governmental barriers to trade, such as tariffs and quotas. As shipping costs decrease, it becomes feasible (economical) to specialize across countries; so, for example, electronic goods are often designed in the U.S. but manufactured in China, Taiwan, or Korea. This specialization leads to increased positive-sum cooperative transactions. That we sometimes misperceive these trades as being harmful is due to zero-sum thinking and perhaps to xenophobia (fear of foreigners).

Of course, specialization would not be feasible without extensive markets. That is because as people become increasingly specialized, they also become increasingly dependent on others for goods and services. Again, I will use myself as an example. I am an economist. As such, I teach economics, I write about economics, and I sometimes consult on economic issues. None of these activities produces any tangible products. Of course, I want lots of products, both for work and for consumption. I want food, clothing, shelter, computers, paper, ink, books, a smartphone. How do I get them? I get them through a hugely complex web of exchanges with people all over the world, people I will never meet and whose existence I know about only in the most general sense. (I know that someone must have sewn my shirt, but I don't know anything about this person, including even what country he or she is from. I may know that it was inspected by Number 16, but that does not tell me much.) The market has enabled a massive web of cooperation that enables extensive specialization and massive wealth. Specialization is the essence of cooperation.

Why is there specialization? The simplest answer is that specialization makes us more productive and so gives us access to more goods and services. That is, specialization is one of the bases—the most important base—of the positive-sum economy in which we operate. Of course, no central power controls specialization or decides on the level of specialization in an activity in a market economy. Rather, individuals seeking their own welfare will specialize if that increases their income. One role of entrepreneurs in an economy is to perceive ways to increase productivity by increasing specialization in some line of activity (think Henry Ford and the assembly line). As conditions merit, specialization will naturally increase and lead to increases in output.

How does specialization increase productivity? There are several channels through which this increase occurs.

First, specialization can enable us to do those things we do best. If I lived in a society where 95 percent of the people were farmers, I would probably be a farmer as well. But I don't think I would have been a very good farmer. I know I am not a good cook or housekeeper. On the other hand, I am a pretty good economist. Because the U.S. economy has sufficient degrees of specialization, I can make my living by specializing in economics and trading (again, indirectly) with farmers for the food I need and with others for household services.

By specializing, we can get better at those things we do. A potential farmer can major in agriculture in college, spend time working on the farm and learning about planting cycles and pest control, read specialized magazines aimed at farmers, work for a farm, and generally become very good at being a farmer. Moreover, a farmer in Illinois will learn about different crops and weather conditions and pests than will a farmer in Alabama. Modern farmers are much better farmers than farmers in the past, who might have had to spend time making some of their own tools and perhaps preparing some of their own food for sale in ways that are now done by other specialists. Moreover, they would have grown a wider variety of crops than a modern farmer; that is, they would have been less specialized. On the other hand, by specializing in economics, I can be a much better economist than someone who must teach both economics and moral philosophy (although Adam Smith did a pretty good job).

Another source of gains from specialization is the savings from not having to spend time changing tasks. A farmer can spend all his working time on the farm; I can spend all of mine at the university. There is no need to travel from one task to another.

There are also gains from specialized machinery. An assembly line is made of many machines, each doing a narrow task. In a custom machine shop, there are relatively unspecialized tools, and each is used for several tasks. As output of a particular product increases, machinery to make that part becomes more and more specialized, so that in an automobile plant there are huge expensive machines specialized to stamping out one metal part, which they do over and over.

More recently, for many of us, machinery has become less specialized. Smartphones have replaced telephones, cameras, GPS machines, books, e-readers, and other specialized devices. Computers have replaced typewriters, calculators, adding machines, and many other machines. But in these cases, the level of specialization has moved from hardware to software so that particular tasks are performed by specialized apps or programs.

In addition to increased productivity, there is another benefit to specialization. As specialization increases, there are more types of jobs in the economy. This creates a benefit to individuals because it is easier to find a job that meets one's individual preferences and abilities. The Bureau of Labor Statistics indicates that there are tens of thousands of job titles in the U.S. economy. Thus, as specialization increases, it becomes easier to find a desirable niche for each individual, which leads to an increase in human happiness.

Specialization also affects personal consumption. Think of the stereotypical pioneer family. The wife would sew clothes, perhaps from skins of animals killed by the husband. (Sorry for the gender stereotypes, but they are accurate.) The family would grow its own food in a small plot. The local general store of itinerant merchants would sell some inputs (needles for sewing, pots for cooking, guns and ammunition for shooting game) but families were relatively self-sufficient—that is, relatively unspecialized.

A big change was the advent of catalog stores, primarily Sears and Montgomery Ward. These stores enabled rural farmers to participate in a much larger market, and so become more specialized and less self-sufficient. The wife no longer needed to sew her own clothes—she could purchase them, perhaps providing more time for farming and so enabling her to sell some crops on the market, so that the buyers of these crops could devote more time to their own specialty. The process continues—restaurants and food takeout or delivery enterprises enable people to spend less time on food preparation. The entities mentioned above such as Craigslist and Fiverr enable people to hire out additional small tasks, and so free up more time for productive activity ("I can find someone to cut the grass so I may go to work on Saturday") or leisure.

But while the economy depends on cooperation, competition is also important. In the next chapter, I discuss competition.

CHAPTER 4

COMPETITION

One of the main points I want to make in this chapter is that the way in which economists use the term "competition" is different from the way that noneconomists use the term and that this difference leads to a lot of mischief. But before I begin this analysis, I want to make two different points. I want to discuss the fundamental nature of competition and the importance of competition.

We think of firms competing with other firms. Firms want to sell more, or gain market share, or put their rivals out of business. On the buying side, firms want to hire the best workers or gain access to the best sources of supply.

But here is the important point: To the extent that firms are competing, they are competing for *the right to cooperate*. If a firm wants to sell more than its rivals, this means that it wants to cooperate with more consumers. If it wants to hire the best workers, that means that it wants to cooperate with those workers. If it offers better terms (say, lower prices) than its competitors, it does so to gain more consumers with whom to cooperate, and the ultimate benefit of this competition goes to the consumers. As a leading marketing text describes the process, "Building profitable customer relationships requires satisfying target consumer needs *better than competitors do*" (Kotler and Armstrong, 2010, p. 547).

We often lose sight of this important truth. We may focus on the "competitive battle" between two firms because tales of such competition and rivalry are often exciting. Newspapers, business magazines, and books report these stories as if they are war stories. As we see below, when economists discuss oligopoly (a market structure with a "few" firms), they also focus on the interaction between those firms. But in all cases, the ultimate target of the competition and the ultimate beneficiary is the consumer.

Second, let us consider the importance of competition. We often hear praise of the competitive economy or of free competition. Economists, and particularly free market economists such as myself, are fond of statements of this sort, as are many pro-market politicians and newscasters. This is correct: competition, and particularly free competition, is very important to an economy. But only one part of the competitive process is actually beneficial. That is the right of free entry into a market. As long as entry is free, then we will achieve all the benefits of competition.

Competition is not the purpose of an economy. Competition is a tool. To the extent that we can say that the economy has a purpose, the purpose or goal of an economy is cooperation through exchange: transactions. Transactions are what lead to the benefits of the market. Benefits are realized when goods move to higher-valued uses or when both parties gain from some exchange. Competition through free entry is a tool that leads to the most efficient set of exchanges and maximizes the benefits of the exchanges, but it is the process of exchange that generates the benefits of the market. It is in this sense that emphasis on competition is misleading; the fundamental nature of the economy is cooperative, not competitive. Competition means that transactions occur on the best possible feasible terms (for everyone, buyers and sellers) and are between the best set of parties, but the benefit comes from the transaction. Competition is more exciting, but cooperation does the work.

Economists and Market Structure

To understand the difference between cooperation and competition, we must first understand how economists use the term "competition." To economists, competition is a term of art. That is, it is a term used with a special meaning that is not the same as its use in general discourse. Indeed, the confusion between the way in which economists use the term and the use of the term in normal discourse is one of the major themes of this book. In textbooks, the major conditions for "perfect competition" or "pure competition" are many buyers and sellers, free entry and exit, and complete information. Confusion arises because individuals untrained in economics (and even some with economic training) confuse economists' use of the word "competition" with the normal use of the term. In particular, in the market structure that economists call "perfect competition," *there is no competition* in the sense that noneconomists use the term. No firm is competing with another. None of the firms is trying to be first or to be more successful or larger than the other firms. No firm cares in any sense about any of the other firms.

Pure competition is one market structure. To understand the use of competition by economists, we must look at the theory of market structures. Economists define market structures in terms of the number of firms in the market. There may be "many," "few," or one. I consider each. I then consider some additional aspects of competition.

"Many" Firms: Perfect Competition

Economists' favorite market structure is one with many firms and free entry, called "pure" or "perfect" competition. The definition hinges on the meaning of "many." Economists define "many" as so many that each firm ignores the behavior of others and behaves as if other firms have no effect on its profits or prices. This explains why there is no competition in this market structure, even though it is called perfect competition. Another way of saying the same thing is that in this market structure, each firm takes price as given and assumes that no matter how much or how little it sells, it can have no influence on price. This is because the sales of each firm are an infinitesimal part of the entire market.

For an example, consider an agricultural market, such as the market for corn. There are hundreds of thousands of corn farmers. Any given farmer assumes (correctly) that his or her behavior will not influence the market price of corn. Similarly, no individual farmer pays any attention to the behavior of any other farmer. Farmer Brown does not care how much Farmer Jones plants because the market price of corn will be independent of each of their actions. About one hundred million acres are planted in corn in the U.S., and a large farm will be perhaps five hundred acres, so that there may be over two hundred thousand corn farms in the U.S. Each farmer is therefore a miniscule fraction of the total. This is what we mean by "many." If Farmer Brown switches the back forty (acres) from soybeans to corn, this will have no effect on the price of corn or on Farmer Jones.

How do firms behave in this market structure? Each firm takes the market price as a given and must adapt to that price. (In an agricultural market or in other markets with a lag between beginning production and sales, the price is the forecast price when the crop will be harvested or the product will be sold.) We may view the adaptation as being in two parts. First, the firm must decide whether to be in the market at all. For a corn farmer, this is the first planting decision: Should I plant corn at all, or stick to soybeans? This is the condition of free entry and exit: Firms are free to enter the market or to leave, by varying crops. Second, if the farm is to plant corn, it must decide how much corn to plant. Price governs both decisions. If farmers anticipate a high corn price, then more farms will plant corn, and each will plant more corn. If they expect a low price, they will plant less corn and more soybeans or alfalfa instead, and some will plant no corn at all. The perfect information assumption is that all farmers know the price of corn and the cost of growing corn; this assumption can be most easily relaxed, and I will assume that sufficient information is available to drive the market, but it need not be "perfect" in the economists' sense. As long as errors in forecasting are unbiased (as many farmers assume too high a price as assume too low a price), the market will move in the correct direction.

Markets such as this have certain very nice features, which is why economists like them. (I ignore any effects of government policies on the market.) One nice feature of competition is that price is driven down to the lowest feasible level, down to the level of costs. (Technically, at long-run equilibrium, price is equal to marginal cost, which is also equal to long-run average total cost. This means that firms are covering all costs but making neither excess profits nor losses.) If price is high (above the appropriately measured cost), so that planting corn pays better than planting soybeans, more corn will be planted because more farmers will enter that market. But if more corn is planted, then the market price will move downward. This process will continue until the returns from corn (and soybeans, and all other crops) are the same. Economists say that when this happens, firms are making "normal" returns. Although firms would like to earn more than this normal return, market forces are such that they cannot. Consumers benefit because they are getting corn for the lowest possible price. Conversely, if the price of corn is too low, so that farmers are not covering their costs, then farmers will leave the market or plant less corn, driving the price up until again returns are equalized across crops. This is why I said that competition means transactions take place at the best possible price.

If price is too low and some firms must leave the market, which firms will leave? The firms with the highest costs—the most inefficient firms at growing corn—will be the first to leave. (These may just be the firms for which some other crop is most appealing so that the opportunity cost of corn is highest.) Conversely, what if price is above equilibrium so that potential entrants can make profits? Who will make the greatest profits and so be the first to enter? It will be the most efficient firm that is not currently in the market, the firm with the lowest costs of planting corn. Entry will occur until the last firm to enter makes only an infinitesimal amount over costs. In other words, for any market price, entry and exit will mean that the firms in the market will be the most efficient (lowest-cost) set of firms. The result of this entry and exit is that cooperation (exchange) takes place on the best possible terms. That is, entry and exit lead to the result that cooperation—transactions—take place on the best possible terms for consumers. Moreover, the firms in the industry will be the set of firms with the lowest costs for that level of production. So the result of what economists call "perfect competition" is in fact "perfect cooperation:" cooperation on the best terms for consumers. It is in this sense that competition assures that the correct firms will be the ones in the market.

A second nice feature of markets such as this is that they are responsive to consumer preferences. For example, assume that for some reason consumers want more corn. Perhaps it is a good movie season and so more people want popcorn. (Movies and popcorn are what economists call "complementary" goods, goods that are consumed together.) Then the immediate price of corn will increase, and this will lead farmers to plant more corn. The effect will be twofold. First, there will be more corn, which is what consumers want. Second, the price will fall from its immediate peak, as more corn will be available. (Whether it will move all the way back to the original price is an important question, but not one we need consider here.)

From our perspective, the most interesting fact about this market structure is that *there is no competition.* We economists call this perfect competition, but as noneconomists use the term, there is no competition. Since each firm takes the behavior of other firms as given and ignores them, firms are not competing with one another in any meaningful sense. Prices and quantities are affected by decisions about which crops and how much of each to plant, but these decisions are made independently by each firm, and there is no interaction and so no competition. Firms are out to maximize their own profits independently of the behavior of any other firm. More generally, economists say that entry and exit decisions drive the market: Do I plant corn or not? The important characteristic of such markets is that at equilibrium, returns on capital are equalized across all markets.

In sports—the origin of the term "competition"—each player is acutely aware of all the others, and the goal of each player is to beat the others. But in pure competition, each player is completely indifferent to all the others. It is in this sense that economists say that there is no "competition" (in the normal sense of the word) in pure "competition" (in the economists' sense of the word).

This analysis points out what is the crux of the problem I am addressing in this book. Economists like "perfect competition" because of its equilibrium characteristics. But as laymen use the term "competition," there is no competition in the economists' competitive market. That is, firms do not attempt to get more business from other firms; they do not attempt to drive other firms out of business. They do not pay any attention at all to other firms in the market. No firm cares if it is larger or more profitable than any other firm, or if another firm changes its behavior. The term "competition" was borrowed from sports, but the competition that economists like is totally unlike sports competition. In sports competition, only relative position (win or lose) matters; in economic pure competition, it does not matter at all.

So economists in textbooks, classrooms, blogs, and policy discussions advocate something we call "competition," but when noneconomists hear us, they think of something else altogether. We economists think in terms of small firms ignoring one another; laymen think in terms of firms trying to gain market share from others and trying to put them out of business. We do not clarify the distinction enough, so that even students who have taken our courses may be confused. This is the key area in which economists actually sabotage markets by making them appear less desirable.

Here is a point. Economists use the term "profits" differently than others do. We subtract opportunity costs (foregone earnings) from actual earning, so that if a firm is earning only a return on capital, we say that the firm is earning zero profits; an accountant would say that the firm is earning significant profits because the return on capital, which to economists is a cost, is profit to accountants (and tax collectors). In teaching economics, we make a major point of explaining this distinction. We discuss at length the difference between accounting profits and economic profits. But we do not do the same thing with respect to competition. Our definition of competition is just as different from the normal meaning as is true of profits. But we explain one difference in detail and ignore the other.

Our use of the term "price discrimination" is similar to our use of competition: Economists' use of the term is not the same as use by noneconomists. To an economist, price discrimination occurs whenever it is feasible to separate consumers by elasticity (price sensitivity) at a reasonable cost and profitable to charge them different prices. It has nothing to do with racial or most other characteristics of buyers, and there is no malice in the behavior of a firm engaging in price discrimination; the behavior is purely about making money. Moreover, in many cases price discrimination is a socially beneficial practice. But to noneconomists, the term "discrimination" has negative connotations, so much so that firms engaging in price discrimination go to great lengths to use other terms, such as "dynamic pricing."

Economics is not unique among sciences in using terms in specific ways that differ from nonscientific usage. For example, to laymen, "steel" is a hard, silver-colored metal. But to a metallurgist, steel is a complex mixture of iron and other elements in particular proportions, depending on the type of steel. To a layman, "germs" cause disease, but to a doctor or biologist, there are numerous types of bacteria and viruses, and many of them are helpful. To a layman, "genetic engineering" is some new and perhaps scary technology, but biologists know that humans have been practicing genetic engineering since they began breeding plants and animals. But for most sciences, the fact that the technical vocabulary differs in meaning from normal usage of terms has no particular policy implications, just as a belief in a flat earth has no particular policy implications. Unfortunately, for economists and for economic policy, this difference in the use of terms by economists and others does have important consequences.

One Firm: Monopoly

A market with a single seller is called a monopoly. The important result about monopoly is immediate: Since there is only one firm, the firm is not competing with any other firm. The monopolist is still constrained in his or her behavior, but the constraint is from the demand side of the market, not from competition with other firms. It is sometimes said that a monopolist "can charge whatever he wants." This is true in a trivial sense, but the monopolist cannot sell all that he wants if he charges whatever he wants. At any given price, the amount that a monopolist can sell is limited by his demand curve; if he charges more, he can sell less. For a given demand curve and a given set of costs, there is only one price that maximizes the monopolists' profits, and a monopoly will generally do its best to figure out what that price is and then charge that price (subject to any regulation). The price can be calculated mechanically once cost and demand conditions are known. Unlike the case in pure competition, the price charged will generally be higher than costs, leading to the monopolist making excess profits—profits over the cost of capital. Moreover, some consumers who would be willing to pay the cost of production of the product, or even something more, will nonetheless not purchase it because the monopoly price is above the amount they would be willing to pay. This leads to a loss in what is called "consumer surplus." This is why economists do not like monopolists as much as we like competitive firms. Of course, there may be reasons for the existence of a monopolist, such as a patent, which may offset the costs of the higher price.

How does a firm become a monopolist in a market? There are several ways. Some are good, some are bad, and some are truly ugly. There are also laws regulating the behavior of monopolists, the "antitrust laws." I will consider these laws later; for now, I note that the term "market" in the first sentence above is a term with a lot of legal baggage. But for now, we can ignore that issue and look at ways of becoming a monopolist. (I also note that a "monopsonist" is a firm with an exclusive right to cooperate with sellers in some market. That is, a monopsonist is the only buyer of some product or service. The results of monopoly analysis apply to monopsonists, in reverse. That is, monopsonists pay too low a price for the monopsonized good, and sellers of the good lose more than the monopsonist gains.)

The Good

There are two good ways to become a monopolist: to be the first to do something new, or to do something so much better (or cheaper) that no one else can compete. In both cases, firms become monopolists because they are doing a better job of cooperating with customers. Creation of new products generates new ways of cooperating. Lowering costs or improving products improves the terms of cooperation. In these cases, consumers of the products benefit from the increased cooperation. Moreover, one of the main drivers of socially useful behavior, such as innovation in technology or inventing new products, is the desire of the firm to become a monopolist. That is, while monopoly may impose short-run costs on the economy in the form of excess prices and lost consumer surplus, it may also have long-run benefits that outweigh these costs.

Be the First

If a firm creates some product, then it is a monopolist because no one else is making that product. In today's world there are many such monopolists. Apple has created many products: the iPod, the iPad, the iPhone smartphone. In each of these markets, Apple was for a time a monopolist, until someone else was able to make a product that would compete with Apple's product for the right to cooperate with customers.

There are several benefits of being first. One is acquiring a patent. This is a legally enforceable right to prevent others from undertaking some action. A patent is an incentive granted by the state to induce agents to provide new ways of cooperating by inventing new products or processes. The trade-off is clear: firms are given short-run rights to exclusive sales and so to higher profits as an incentive to create something new.

In some industries such as pharmaceuticals, patents are essential. This is because a patent covers one particular molecule, and that molecule itself provides some health benefit. Without a patent, anyone could make that molecule and erode the profits of the first firm. This would eliminate incentives to spend time and money to develop the molecule and obtain regulatory approval to sell it in the first place.

In other industries, patents are less essential, and may even be harmful. This applies to industries such as cellphones and computers where many patents owned by many separate agents are necessary to produce a product. In order to produce a valuable product in such markets, firms must cooperate with one another and allow the use of patents by competitors. Alternatively, firms may engage in expensive and unproductive patent litigation. There are even firms called "patent trolls" that exist solely to buy up patents and charge royalties or engage in litigation with productive firms. The courts, Congress, and regulatory agencies such as the FTC are as I write this trying to restructure patent law to reduce or eliminate these costs. Nonetheless, overall, patents are very useful for promoting new products and new forms of cooperation.

A second way of benefiting from being first is a "trade secret." Patents provide exclusive protection, but there are two drawbacks from the perspective of the firm. First, to get a patent a firm must disclose the details of the product. Second, patents run out after a fixed time. When the patent runs out, competitors can easily enter the market since the firm has disclosed the details of the product to obtain a patent. (For example, Amazon's patent on "one-click" ordering has recently expired, and others will soon be offering this method of purchase.) For these reasons, firms sometimes decide not to patent their products, but rather to protect them with another legal form of protection, a trade secret. In this case, the firm need not disclose, and the secret can exist as long as the firm can keep it secret. On the other hand, anyone who can figure out what is involved in producing the product can produce it. The best-known example of a product protected by a trade secret is Coca-Cola, which has been around since 1886. Had the company had a patent, it would have long since expired, and the world would be filled with generic cola drinks identical to Coke. Of course, others such as Pepsi have been free to do the best they could at copying the Coke formula since it is not patent-protected.

A third benefit is what economists call "first mover advantage." This means that the first firm in some market often obtains an advantage by virtue of being first. Consumers get used to the product, networks of users and associated products may build up, and the firm may be in the best position to continue improving the product. The firm has learned how to produce the product, and costs tend to go down over time as internal production processes improve, so the cost advantage of being first may persist. All of this may provide sufficient profits to create incentives for innovation. In recent times, Apple has been a poster firm for this benefit. The iPod, iPhone, and iPad have all been the first in their markets, and, while there are many arguably equal or better substitutes now available, Apple still has a significant advantage in these markets. Similarly, Amazon's Echo was the first smart speaker, and while there are now many competitors, Amazon is still benefiting from being first.

What is relevant in many modern markets is what are called "network effects." A network effect is said to exist when the value of some good or service depends on the number of others using that good or service. Network effects can exist on either the supply side or the demand side of a market. For an example of a demand-side network effect, consider Microsoft Word. I can write papers using any word processing program. But my work is much more valuable, and collaboration is much easier, if others can also read my work and edit it. Thus, Microsoft Word had a competitive advantage over others as it became more popular in the marketplace. For a supply-side network effect, consider smartphone apps. As there are more developers of apps for a given platform, that platform becomes more valuable. But app developers want to sell lots of apps and so have an incentive to develop them for popular platforms. For Apple, network effects through iTunes and through networks of suppliers and app developers have been very important. Many consumers are loyal to Apple as well. Android could compete with Apple because it was developed by Google, which had a good position as the largest network in supplying search.

Be the Best

The other way to obtain market power is to do a better job of cooperating with customers or suppliers than do others. This cooperation may be through lower prices or better services or product selection or, more commonly, some combination of these factors. If a firm can do a better job of cooperating than others, it is traditional to say that it is outcompeting other firms. This is correct if we look horizontally—if we look at other firms in the same market. But if we look vertically—at customers or suppliers—then we would say that the firm is doing a better job of cooperating. Moreover, its position as a monopolist derives from its ability to better cooperate with buyers or sellers.

Here competition (as the term is generally used) is important. A firm can maintain a position of market power only so long as it is indeed the best. Over time other firms will try to do better and therefore grow, and some of them may succeed. In today's world we can see this competition taking place rapidly. Facebook did a better job than Friendster; Microsoft did a better job than Apple until Apple did a better job than Microsoft. Android is competing with Apple. Amazon, Google, and Walmart are currently struggling to increase retail positions. All these are examples of competition. But note that the competition is competition for the right to cooperate with consumers by selling them things they want. At any given time, the firm that does the best job of cooperating with consumers by offering the best array of product characteristics will be the firm that wins the competitive race.

There is another sense in which there may be social benefits from monopolization. This would occur if there are sufficient "economies of scale" in an industry. Economies of scale are said to occur when costs become lower as output increases. If there are sufficient economies of scale, then it might pay one firm to acquire all other firms in a market because this will lower costs of production. Even if it does not pay one firm to become a monopoly, if there are economies of scale, it will sometimes pay to reduce the number of firms in a market to the point where the market might become an oligopoly.

The Bad

A firm may become a monopolist by buying up all the other firms in the industry. If there are sufficient economies of scale, this can be useful because being larger will lower costs. But in some industries there are neither economies nor diseconomies of scale over a wide range of output. That is, in some industries cost of output is independent of size of the firm over a wide range of sizes. Small firms are no more and no less efficient than large firms. In such an industry, market structure (number of firms in the industry) is indeterminate—the industry may have many firms, or a few, or only one. It is in this structure that the antitrust laws are most important. A firm may attempt to become a monopolist solely to raise prices, with no benefit to consumers.

Some people think that a firm may engage in "predation," activities aimed at driving its competitors out of business. To these people, it appears that cutting price below costs until rivals are bankrupt and then raising price is an efficient tactic for the firm. Economists generally think this mostly does not pay and is very uncommon. The predating firm is larger and sells more than its rivals, and so it will lose more money than will the smaller firms during the predation period. Indeed, the smaller firms can simply shut down temporarily and allow the predator to lose even more money by supplying the entire market at a loss. Also, if the predator were to succeed, then when it tried to raise prices, others could enter and erode these prices. It is for these reasons that the courts try to determine if an alleged predator would be able to recoup the costs of the predation; most commonly, they find that the alleged predator would not be successful and so would not engage in the behavior in the first place. Nonetheless, laymen (noneconomists) believe that predation is much more common than it actually is. This belief is one consequence of describing the economy as competitive. Harming your rival (perhaps by tripping him) may be an effective way to win a competitive race, but it is not an effective tactic to be a better cooperator.

However, in some circumstances it might pay to purchase all competitors solely to become a monopolist. This is bad because the monopolist does not do anything to improve the terms of cooperation to gain its position and is able to increase price (make cooperative terms worse) after gaining its monopoly position. But while this might in theory occur, in advanced economies the antitrust laws make this behavior very difficult or impossible, and it is not a common way of obtaining monopoly power. Indeed, the antitrust authorities may be more likely to erroneously penalize efficient acquisitions based on economies of scale rather than to allow inefficient acquisitions aimed at gaining monopoly power. Moreover, if a firm did do this in an industry with no significant economies of scale, then as soon as it raised price, others would enter, either to make profits or to sell out at a profit to the monopolist.

The Ugly

One highly socially inefficient but sometimes privately effective way to become a monopolist is to enlist the government to keep out competitors. I call this the ugly because it says nothing about the ability of the firm to cooperate with consumers (although it does imply the ability to cooperate with the government), and once government grants a monopoly, it is very difficult for it to overturn it. Exclusive licenses can create monopolies. For example, many "public utilities" (water, natural gas, traditional telephone service, cable TV, buses, mail delivery, taxicabs, railroads) have been monopolists because the government has granted them exclusive licenses or because the government runs the business itself. The traditional argument has been that the industry is a "natural monopoly" (only room for one efficient-sized firm because of economies of scale) and the government therefore allowed a monopoly and then regulated it. In many cases, such as telephony, breaking up what was thought to be a natural monopoly (AT&T) has led to increased competition, in this case from numerous cellphone suppliers.

Government regulation sometimes creates inefficient market structures that are not technically monopolies. This is when government limits entry into some market, as by licensing. Under these circumstances, there are many sellers but entry is not possible because of licensing restrictions. In this market structure, firms can earn positive profits because entry cannot erode these profits. This is common in transportation markets: Many cities limit the number of taxicabs or limousine services. In these markets, the present value of the license is capitalized into the price of the license itself, and licenses can sell for high prices. For example, in New York City, taxi medallions (the tangible form of the license) sold in the past for up to $1 million. As I write this, this entry restriction is creating a market niche for firms such as Uber which can erode the market position of taxicabs. However, Uber, Lyft, and similar firms are having difficulty because they must contend with the existing regulatory structure, which is aimed mainly at protecting the existing taxicab and limousine firms, which in turn have close relationships with the regulators and often the politicians who grant exclusive licenses.

As discussed above, practitioners of many occupations are also licensed, and this also limits entry and increases prices. The number of jobs for which licenses are required has increased, and it is now estimated that 25 percent of U.S. jobs require a license. While entry is possible in these markets, it is limited, and so those in the industry can earn excess returns. These excess returns may be used to hire lobbyists to maintain entry limitations and perhaps seek additional benefits.

In all these cases, the government has intervened to limit possibilities of cooperation and has correspondingly harmed consumers. By requiring a license, the government has eliminated other non-licensed potential cooperators. But the bottom line for us is that *in a monopoly there is competition to become a monopolist, but no competition once the monopoly is created.* When economists refer to the benefits of competition, they do not mean competition to become a monopolist through government regulation.

Few Firms: Oligopoly

Finally, if there are few firms in the market, then there can be competition in the sense that laymen use the term. Each firm observes the behavior of others, and each firm responds to the behavior of others.

These responses may be in terms of price, quantity, product characteristics, or advertising. For a nice example where responses play out every night on TV, think of the cellphone market, where there are four major firms. Firms compete on price (for phones and for plans), quality (of phones and of networks), advertising, and contractual terms. We have finally found our market structure with competition. Moreover, many markets are exactly of this form. There are relatively few purely competitive markets and relatively few monopolies, but oligopolies are everywhere.

The theory of pure competition and the theory of monopoly are straightforward because there is no competition in those markets and so no need to factor in human behavior. In each case there are demand and cost curves, and optimal (profit maximizing) behavior can be mechanically computed from the data using standard tools of economics or of mathematics.

This is not so for oligopoly. Here, there is a lot of room for strategy and for human behavior. Each firm must consider how it should respond to each move by its rivals and what their likely response is to its behaviors. Moreover, responses can be in different dimensions: If Verizon improves its network, AT&T can improve its network as well, but it can also improve its phones (the iPhone) or change its pricing. Game theory is the branch of economics that studies actions and reactions of firms in market structures where these factors are important, and the results can be complicated.

But let us step back and look at this competition. For what are firms competing? Fundamentally, they are competing to sell products to consumers. But a sale is a cooperative act. Thus, in an oligopoly, *firms are competing for the right to cooperate with consumers.*

This competition is essential for a well-functioning market. By competing, firms force price to lower levels and force product improvements. The praise that commentators heap on competition is not misguided. Competition is very important and is the driving force for efficiency in an economy. Indeed, even competitive firms might seek some new technology in order to become monopolists. Economies without competition are stagnant and provide few consumer benefits. If we can convert monopolies to competitive markets (as, for example, by creating a voucher system for education and so eliminating the public school monopoly, or by privatizing the post office) we can provide real benefits to consumers. By no means do I want to be read as downplaying the importance of competition, or else I will be eliminated from the guild of economists.

In actual markets, we are now seeing new forms of cooperation-based competition. Apple started off as a computer manufacturer, Google as a search engine, Amazon as a bookseller, and Facebook as a social network. But these firms are expanding into one another's space. They are doing this by creating components that cooperate with one another to give consumers and sellers one place to find many cooperative services. For example, Amazon tried to develop and sell a phone, but it was unsuccessful. Instead, it developed the Amazon Echo, a general-purpose voice-activated machine which does many things, but it is also very useful for selling Amazon products, and Amazon came up with several variants of this product. Google developed the Android operating system to compete with Apple in selling goods online, which gives it a presence in phones and many other markets, and it increasingly physically manufactures products. Because of the success of the Amazon Echo, Google developed the Google Home, a similar product. Google is having some difficulty competing with Amazon because of Amazon's first-mover advantage for this product. Apple's iTunes, originally a music service, now competes with Amazon and Google in selling digital content of all sorts. In all these examples and many more, firms are engaging in this "platform competition" by creating components that work together to give consumers a better experience in cooperating with suppliers.

But while competition is very important, we must understand its role. Competition is not the purpose of an economy. To the extent that an economy can be said to have a purpose, the purpose is to generate consumer welfare. That is, the reason that societies allow free markets and capitalist or competitive systems is because they generate benefits for consumers. The benefits are called "consumer surplus" by economists because this is a measure of the benefits that consumers gain over and above what they must pay for a good or service. This surplus is created through exchange, which is a cooperative act. Competition is a tool for improving the cooperation that occurs in markets. By competing, Verizon, AT&T, Sprint, and T-Mobile provide real benefits to consumers, but those benefits are not realized until transactions occur. The transactions are the source of the benefits; competition is the tool for generating these benefits.

Collusion: Harmful Cooperation

There is also cooperation in oligopolies. However, this cooperation is not the useful positive-sum form of cooperation we have been discussing. Rather, firms in oligopolies may cooperate with one another to raise prices and harm consumers. We call this sort of cooperation "collusion" or "conspiracy in restraint of trade," and the firms that engage in the behavior a "cartel" (to be distinguished from a drug cartel, which seems to mean a single large illegal firm). Essentially, firms engaging in this behavior are attempting to obtain monopoly-like profits by cooperating to behave like a monopolist.

Much of the analysis of oligopoly by economists is analysis of this cooperation. There are two opposing tendencies of firms in a small-numbers situation. First, if the firms can cooperate (collude), they can increase their joint total profits. Second, however, is the incentive for each firm to cheat on any collusive agreement. If firms have agreed to raise price and limit output, then any one firm can make even more if it can lower its price by a little bit and increase its sales at the expense of other firms in the industry. Because all firms have this incentive, collusive agreements are fragile and may break of their own weight. All oligopolies are subject to this tension unless they can enlist government to enforce their agreement.

I also want to point out that in many economics textbooks, the main usage of the term "cooperation" is to refer to such inefficient agreements. Such cooperation is harmful. As a result, students may come to believe that cooperation in an economy is harmful, without being told that all markets actually run on cooperation. This is a further example of the usage of words by economists undermining public understanding of the benefits of a market system.

Antitrust

The antitrust laws try to limit this inefficient behavior in three ways. First, these laws outlaw any formal agreement by firms to collude ("contracts or conspiracies in restraint of trade"). By outlawing them, they make it impossible for would-be colluders to use the courts to enforce their illegal agreements. This also means that the agreements must be secret and that efforts to enforce the agreements cannot be obvious. All these factors make it more difficult for firms to collude successfully. Here is a case where competition undermines undesirable cooperation to the benefit of consumers.

Second, much of the regulation of mergers is aimed at making it more difficult for firms to reach a position where such collusion is possible. The antitrust laws require all firms to notify the government (the Federal Trade Commission or the Department of Justice) of mergers over a certain size, and these agencies will examine mergers to determine if they believe them to be anticompetitive. Mergers are held to be anticompetitive if they give one firm too much market power or if they create a movement toward oligopoly which will make successful collusion easier. If so, the antitrust authorities can suggest changes in the terms of the merger ("fix it first") or sue to stop the merger. (Full disclosure: For some years, I was an economic consultant in the anti-trust business, and I made my living by analyzing such mergers with an eye toward showing that they were not anticompetitive. Since I do believe that most mergers are not anticompetitive, I was comfortable with this job.)

Third, collusion itself is illegal, and firms can be punished for colluding. The punishment may be in the form of a fine ("treble" damages, three times the profit from the collusion) or even jail time for executives. Moreover, victims of collusion can sue in civil court for treble damages. Because this form of cooperation is harmful, in some economics textbooks cooperation itself gets a bad name. In these books, the most important discussion of cooperation may be in terms of cooperating in order to collude. But this form of cooperation is only a small fraction of the total cooperation in an economy, and most cooperation is beneficial.

CHAPTER 5

LESSONS FROM COMPETITION AND COOPERATION

As we shift our view of the economy from competition to cooperation, our perspective on behaviors and outcomes changes. In this chapter, I discuss some of these changes.

Winners and Losers

When there is competition, there are winners and losers. We often feel sorry for the losers. There are several reasons for this sympathy. We may feel that the winners had some sort of unfair advantage (not a "level playing field"). Experimental evidence shows that noneconomists place much more weight on fairness than do economists. Moreover, the concept of fairness is open-ended and not well-defined, so it would be easy to think of winners as having an unfair advantage, perhaps proven by the fact that they have won. We may just root for the "underdog." The behavioral economists have taught us that we put more weight on losses than on gains (called "loss aversion"), and so we may feel greater sympathy for the losers than we feel joy for the winners. We may view the winners as monopolists and so resent them. If we view the process as competitive, this leads us to structure the problem in a way that focuses our attention on these losers.

In analyzing the attitudes of laypersons with respect to market outcomes, we must realize that most people really do not pay much attention to these issues. Since you are reading this book, you are much more concerned with economic and political outcomes than is the average person. It makes sense for people not to pay attention to these issues since they cannot have any effect on them. People are said to be "rationally ignorant" of much political activity. But since this is so, a seemingly minor change in terminology (from "competition" to "cooperation") could have a disproportionate impact on their thinking.

Although these feelings of sympathy for the unsuccessful firm are natural, they are misguided when we are talking about competition among firms for our business. Some of the reason for these feelings is because we misunderstand the nature of business competition. Businesses are not competing with one another to "win." A marketplace is not a race. Rather, businesses are competing for the right to sell us something. The winner is the business that does the best job of selling us what we want to buy. The unsuccessful firms in a market are unsuccessful because they have not done as good a job of cooperating with customers. The winners in competition have won because they have given us, the consumers, what we want; the losers lose because they have not.

This point is very important. A successful business is one that does the best job of satisfying consumer demands. This means that it offers the combination of price, quality, and terms that consumers most prefer. If we realize that transactions are cooperative, then the successful firm is the best cooperator. Conversely, firms that do not succeed do not offer as good a deal to consumers. A firm that fails does not fail because a more successful firm has harmed it in some way. Rather, a firm fails because it has not done as good a job of satisfying consumer demands. It is consumers who ultimately determine the fate of firms. In general, we should be grateful to successful firms and at best indifferent to failures. The successful firms are providing benefits to humans; the failures are not. The antitrust authorities in the U.S. understand this point when they say that "antitrust protects competition, not competitors," but this principle is sometimes lost in public discussions, and sometimes even in antitrust itself. Complaints from competitors are an important driver of antitrust. But competitors are actually complaining that more successful firms are doing a better job of cooperating with consumers.

In general, when a successful firm harms a competitor, it does so by offering better terms to consumers, and so it increases social welfare. Consider an extreme example—what is called "predation"—charging a low price to drive competitors out of business with the intent of increasing prices later. As I mentioned above, this behavior is unusual because it is very difficult to make up any losses, to "recoup" the losses suffered during the predation period. However, that does not stop unsuccessful rivals from claiming that they are suffering from predation when they lose a competitive battle. In the U.S., the laws regulating international trade even have specific remedies for an American firm allegedly harmed by successful foreign competitors. These laws harm consumers and are generally very harmful. They are a result of what I have called the "ugly": businesses getting the government to protect them from more efficient competitors. In the past, the antitrust laws sometimes penalized a firm for being too successful as a competitor. Some of this still occurs, as when the government brought an antitrust action against Microsoft and investigated Google, both of which are very successful cooperators. European antitrust authorities are apparently using the antitrust laws to punish American firms and benefit European firms, rather than to benefit European consumers.

In these cases, doctrines of competition are being misused. A successful firm is providing benefits to consumers by cooperating on better terms than the unsuccessful firm offers. If the unsuccessful firm can induce the government to penalize the successful firm, then it is contributing to a loss of economic welfare because it is eliminating or punishing a successful cooperator. Like a magician distracting us, so the unsuccessful firm is focusing our attention on "unfair" competition, when the real action is in the successful cooperation that is occurring. Unfortunately, by overstressing competition and ignoring cooperation, we economists are acting like the magician's beautiful assistant (though in many cases we are not as good-looking).

Note that the fact that an entrepreneur has succeeded says nothing about the moral worth of that person. It may be that the entrepreneur was hardworking, honest, open, kind to employees and puppies, and generally a very nice person. (This is how he or she will be portrayed in a corporate biography.) But the person may be lazy, nasty, yell at employees, kick the dog, and generally be a true SOB. (For example, Henry Ford was a vicious anti-Semite, but he still provided tremendous benefits to all consumers, including Jews.) None of this matters. What matters is that a successful entrepreneur provides goods that consumers value and want to buy and does so at a price and cost that allows the firm to prosper. This is the benefit provided by a successful businessperson.

Here is another point. Successful entrepreneurs will sometimes engage in charitable activities under the rubric of "giving back." This is fine; the wealth earned by a successful person belongs to that person, and the owner should feel free to spend it however he or she desires, including giving it away. Moreover, charities funded by the wealthy often do a lot of good; the Bill & Melinda Gates Foundation (with contributions from Warren Buffett) has saved literally millions of lives in Third World countries. (Other foundations may not provide as many benefits.)

But the terminology of "giving back" gives a false and even harmful impression. It implies that by making money, the wealthy person has taken something from society and therefore has an obligation to give something back. In fact, if we keep in mind that the successful entrepreneur has succeeded by satisfying consumer desires, then there is no moral obligation to give anything back. Bill Gates in creating and running Microsoft contributed greatly to the computer revolution, which has provided huge benefits to everyone. His earnings, while astronomical, were merely a small fraction of the benefits that consumers have derived from his activities in the form of consumer surplus. It is fine that Mr. Gates has been so generous with his time and money and has performed many useful tasks through his foundation. But if he kept all his money and spent it on himself and his family (probably impossible, given the amounts involved), he would still have created huge benefits for all of us.

If we discuss the market process in terms of cooperation, many of these misguided feelings would be reduced or eliminated. Rather than referring to successful firms as being the best competitors, we would call them the best cooperators. We would view unsuccessful firms as unsuccessful cooperators. Cooperation is a win-win situation. If we call the market process the cooperative process and referred to "free cooperative markets," we would focus on the gains from market behavior rather than on the losses. Mr. Gates and other philanthropists would be viewed as continuing their beneficial activities in another forum. ("I decided that I could do more good by concentrating on giving away my earnings rather than by continuing to improve the computer industry.")

Not Just Consumers: Other Markets

So far, I have been discussing markets for consumer goods. But we can tell similar stories for other markets. Important classes of markets are markets for inputs into the production process. I will discuss labor markets and capital markets. But markets for inputs are driven by markets for output. That is, a firm will hire a worker or borrow capital for the purpose of producing goods that can be sold to consumers. Intermediate goods, such as factory machinery or trucks, are also valued because they can contribute to producing goods for consumers. Economists say that the demand for factors is "derived" demand, derived from the ultimate purpose of producing goods and services for consumers.

Labor Markets

Labor markets are the essence of cooperation. Firms cannot produce goods and services without workers to do the work, and workers must produce something to generate income to survive. The production process is an explicitly cooperative process. However, as in other markets, our language sometimes leads us to miss this cooperation.

Marx taught that all value is created by labor (the "labor theory of value") and that capitalists "exploited" workers. Marxism has been shown to be an incorrect and extremely harmful theory of markets (see Soviet Union), but in some quarters, Marxist thinking remains, and some view firms as exploiting workers. Even non-Marxists may unconsciously harbor some remnants of Marxist thought. Sometimes politicians use rhetoric that emphasizes what appears to be exploitation.

Labor unions represent workers in their dealings with firms. While some of this interaction is cooperative, at times (particularly around contract negotiations) the rhetoric of unions may become anti-firm and may stress the conflict between workers and firms. As I have indicated, while there is fundamental agreement between buyers and sellers, there is room for disagreement over the price (wage) term in a contract, and at the time of negotiating a contract, this disagreement becomes more prominent. Moreover, while almost all labor contracts are signed without a strike, when there is a strike it becomes newsworthy, and so people may think that labor and firms are more in disagreement than is generally true. Those who believe at some level in the exploitation theory of labor markets may sympathize with the workers.

There is two-sided competition in labor markets. Workers compete for jobs, and firms compete to hire workers. If we consider the hiring side, then an analysis similar to that of consumer markets is relevant. If there are many firms hiring a type of labor, then the market is competitive.

We may view labor markets as matching markets. An efficient market creates the best match between workers and jobs—that is, it finds the fit between workers and jobs that makes cooperation as efficient as possible. In this process, both sides are competing. Workers are competing to get the best job, and firms are competing to hire the best workers. If the market works well, then there is an optimal match. The results are that output is maximized. Of course, as in other markets, no one actually seeks efficiency; workers want the best job they can get, and employers want the best workers they can hire for the wage they are willing to pay. But the result is efficiency (Adam Smith's "invisible hand" again).

Again, notice the result of the competition that exists. The output is transactions between workers and firms. The competitive process improves the terms of these transactions, but the goal of that competition is cooperation that is more efficient. Once more, competition is the tool for achieving better cooperation. Competition leads to the best match described above. Because workers have an ongoing relationship with the firms that hire them, the cooperation between workers and firms is explicit. For example, firms might train workers, and workers might have an expectation of a career with a particular firm. Firms might also invest in pensions for workers. All this implies a long-term cooperative relationship.

Firms that do a better job of cooperating with their employees are like firms that do a better job of cooperating with their customers: they are more likely to survive and thrive. Moreover, efficiency in the labor market means that more goods and services can be produced, which leads to increased output in the product markets. This means more and better transactions, and these transactions are cooperative as well.

The theory of cooperation is also relevant for workers and job seekers. It might seem that the way to be hired and promoted is to be as aggressive and competitive as possible. But the theory discussed here indicates that it is actually better to be cooperative. To be hired, you must convince the employer that you will do a good job of cooperating—with superiors and colleagues, and with suppliers or customers. If an employer thinks that you will always be competitive, the employer is less likely to hire you because you may be viewed as being disruptive.

That the economy is cooperative is also important for career decisions. Some students might not want to go into business because they view business as being too competitive—too "dog eat dog." But if they understand that the economy is actually a mass of cooperation—the most cooperative entity in the world—then they might be willing to change career plans.

Capital Markets

A similar analysis applies to capital markets, although the workings of these markets are more difficult for many of us to understand because, unlike labor markets, few of us have direct experience with both sides of capital markets. We may deposit money in a bank or invest in the stock market, but we do not directly view the other side of this market; that is, we do not see what happens to the money we invest. Moreover, we may tend to view capital markets as driven by "greed." This thinking may be a remnant of the labor theory of value, discussed above. The labor theory of value itself is a relic of primitive thinking. For example, many religions forbid the charging or paying of interest, on the false theory that capital is not productive. Of course, owners of capital and those who invest are greedy in the sense that they are seeking the highest return on the capital. But this is no different from workers seeking the highest wage or consumers seeking the lowest price. Additionally, there are efficiency benefits from capital seeking the highest return because the highest return means that the capital is being used in its most productive alternative.

Fundamentally, the return on capital is a measure of the social productivity of that capital. When investors seek the highest return, they are actually seeking to use the capital in the most productive way possible. As in other markets, the actual use of the capital is associated with a transaction, and the transaction is itself cooperative. As in the case of labor, the relationship between investors and recipients of the investment is cooperative and often ongoing. In fact, some investors—stockholders—may actually become the firm, in the sense that stockholders own the firm. Bondholders and other investors often have long-term relationships with firms in which they invest. Small firms (proprietorships) may be directly owned, so that the supplier of capital owns the firm.

Forms of cooperation between owners of capital and the firms that use that capital may be extremely complex. The point is that suppliers of capital have provided something valuable to the firm, and they want protection from loss. For example, a corporation is a "limited liability" company. This means that investors can lose only the amount they have actually invested. Limited liability protects the other assets of investors. Partners and proprietors, on the other hand, are personally liable for the debts of the firm. The creation of limited liability was an extremely important event for mobilizing capital, for creating possibilities of cooperation between those who had capital to invest and those who could profitably employ the capital. Notice also that both parties had incentives to create this form of investment. Investors wanted protection from losses, but companies wanted a way to guarantee that investors would not be excessively harmed because this was a way to induce owners of capital to invest.

The important characteristic of equilibrium in a "competitive" economy is that the returns on capital in all directions are equalized. This is the function of capital markets. If returns (adjusted for risk) are higher in some areas than in others, then investors, driven by a desire for higher returns, will move money from the lower-paying investments to the areas with the higher-paying investments. This is the mechanism leading to equalization of returns. But there is no explicit competition in this process. Rather, each investor is seeking the highest returns, and users of capital try to convince investors that their capital will be safe and will earn a good return or will earn an expected return commensurate with the level of risk. Because there are huge numbers of potential investors and of demanders of funds, the market for capital is what is traditionally called a competitive market, and, as we saw above, there is no actual competition in a market with a very large number of buyers and sellers.

In the discussion of specialization in Chapter 3, I indicated that specialization requires capital deepening—much behavior is further and further from actual end-use consumers. Machines may build machines that build machines that make final products. But all of these intermediate producers must be paid, and no real money is earned until the final product is purchased. Therefore, there must be some way of paying the intermediate goods producers before any product is sold. Someone must borrow or somehow raise money to pay for this waiting. This is the function of capital markets. They enable producers to compensate suppliers of goods and services before revenue is earned. Moreover, as specialization increases, and markets become deeper, it becomes useful to invent more complex forms of finance to pay these producers and still protect the owners of capital (Kling, 2016).

Horizontal Competition, Vertical Cooperation

In discussing relations between firms, economists distinguish between horizontal and vertical relationships. Firms at the same level of business—say, Ford, General Motors, Chrysler, Toyota, Nissan, Honda, Kia, Hyundai, Mercedes, Audi, and BMW—are horizontally related to one another. Vertical relationships are between firms and their suppliers and their customers. In the auto industry, suppliers would include workers as well as makers of steel, rubber, electrical and electronic components, and other parts. Suppliers would also include office supply companies; sources of capital (lenders and investors); utilities (power, gas, water); and services such as legal, marketing, and other experts. Customers would be auto dealers or consumers themselves, or institutional buyers such as firms and auto rental companies. Increasing specialization means that the number of vertical relationships is continually increasing as tasks become increasingly subdivided.

To the extent that there is competition in an economy, it is at the horizontal level. That is, the auto companies I mentioned above (and any I have omitted) would be competitors. Other firms with a relationship to the industry would cooperate with the auto companies. This means that of all the millions of firms in an economy, a firm will compete with a small number and cooperate with the rest. In other words, cooperation is much more common than is competition.

Workers

Consider yourself as an employee. When you are seeking a job, you compete with other job seekers. Once you have a job, you may compete with other employees for promotions. But in these cases, the number of competitors will generally be rather small. On the other hand, you cooperate with all the other employees of the firm almost all of the time, including those with whom you compete for promotion, through the mechanism of specialization. The firm could not produce without the cooperation of all its employees.

Moreover, consider the nature of the competition for promotion that exists. You are competing by convincing higher-level managers that you are more productive than the other candidates. But what does it mean to be more productive? Since production is a cooperative endeavor, you are competing by convincing the boss that you are a better cooperator. If you are in sales, then you compete with other salesmen and saleswomen by selling more—by doing a better job of cooperating with customers. If you are in production, you compete by getting more output from workers—by doing a better job of cooperating with them. If you are a manager, you must demonstrate that you can work with other managers, which means establishing cooperative relationships with them, and that you can cooperate with those you supervise, by getting them to be productive.

We sometimes think of workers competing by sabotaging their competitors within the firm. This may sometimes happen, but in general it is not a good strategy. It is probably more common in the movies or in the comic strip *Dilbert* than in the real world. If it is detected, the saboteur may be punished and probably fired. Internal sabotage reduces the output and value of the firm, and smart managers will try to deter it and punish it when they observe it. In a well-run firm, you do better by producing more yourself (by being a better cooperator) rather than by harming others.

Here is another example. I am an economist. An economist competes with other economists. (This analysis would apply to other academic disciplines as well.) When first in the job market, he or she may be competing with perhaps twenty-five to seventy-five peers for an initial position. As careers become more specialized, the number of economists with whom one directly competes becomes smaller because there are fewer economists with the same specialties and accomplishments. Economists compete with other economists for space in journals. A few economists may compete for academic honors, such as the Clark award or the Nobel Prize.

But in all these instances, competition is based on the ability to cooperate. In competing for jobs, economists are trying to convince potential employers that they can cooperate with students as teachers, and that they will be able to cooperate with journals by getting papers published and with their colleagues in producing research and teaching. In competing for publication space, they are trying to convince editors that other scholars will find cooperation through citations (the current measure of productivity of scholars, tracked, for example, by Google Scholar) more effective than cooperation with other authors. In competing for awards, again it is based on how successful you have been in inducing others to cooperate with you, perhaps by citing your articles.

Moreover, these forms of competition are indirect. When I submit an article to a journal for publication, I hope that the editor will accept it. (In economics, less than 10 percent of submitted articles are accepted by the leading journals.) I am implicitly competing with other authors for journal space. But in general, I do not know who the other potential authors are, and I do not actively compete against them. (This may not be true if authors are competing for "priority" in some discovery, but that is relatively rare.)

Indeed, the overwhelming interaction of one economist with other economists is cooperative. An economist would have nothing to teach if it were not for the work of innumerable scholars beginning with Adam Smith (who himself cooperated with moral philosophers going back to the Greeks) who have created the body of research that is the basis for teaching. An economist could not do research without this body of work. Citations are a measure of the cooperativeness of scholars. The economists we are most likely to cite and who are most likely to cite us are those in our immediate field of research (for me, law and economics) and those are also the economists with whom we compete for jobs and for journal space. So we cooperate even with those with whom we compete. Moreover, when we economists leave the world of economists, the amount of cooperation increases without bound; we cooperate with universities, with those who fund universities, with granting agencies, with publishers, with computer makers, with students who are our customers, with policymakers, with food providers.

So here is the puzzle. The overwhelming share of our relationships with others is cooperative. A few are sometimes competitive. But economists, who know this, nonetheless have chosen to focus on the small number of competitive relationships. This creates the impression that the economy is based on conflict and competition and misses the huge amount of cooperation that actually exists.

Cooperation in Business

The argument of this book so far is that for any agent (a person, a business, or any other economic actor) there are many more cooperative agents than competitive agents. That is, we cooperate with many more people or businesses than we compete with. Moreover, any business is at any time involved in numerous markets—buying numerous inputs, hiring labor of many sorts, selling products. Most of those markets are large-numbers markets, what economists traditionally call competitive, and what I have been calling cooperative—markets in which there are many players, so that the firm may take price as given. Even in an oligopoly, most transactions take place in cooperative markets. All of this means that it is as important and perhaps more important to concentrate on the cooperative set of markets, and to concentrate on transactions in those markets, rather than focusing on the few small-numbers markets.

Consider the market in which the firm sells, the market in which small-numbers competition is most likely to occur. There are many factors which determine whether a customer will buy from you. One of them is the behavior of competitors, but this is only one factor. Others include aspects of the product offered and the services associated with the product. Amazon is a good example. "Amazon's Leadership Principles, Number 1: Customer Obsession: 'Leaders start with the customer and work backward. They work vigorously to earn and keep customer trust. Although leaders pay attention to competitors, they obsess over customers.'"

Amazon has spent huge efforts concentrating on one aspect of the product—the delivery system. Amazon Prime was an innovation which converted a variable cost to consumers (delivery charge) into a fixed cost (the Prime membership fee.) Once that fee was paid, the marginal cost of any additional item was reduced, and customers would therefore buy more. Amazon has continued to focus on delivery, with shorter and shorter delivery times, associated with additional warehouses and additional efficiencies within warehouses. It is also a leader in experimenting with drones and other speedy delivery technologies. Amazon has also created numerous methods of ordering products—dash buttons, ordering through Echo and its numerous offspring, its own line of tablets which features its own products, and other technologies. In almost all these cases, Amazon was focusing on the "customer" and not on competitors. That is, it was focusing on the cooperative transaction and not on the competitive aspect of business.

This principle sets forth clearly the topic of this section: the distinction between competition and cooperation in business (and more generally in many life decisions). The thesis set forth in this book is consistent with Amazon's philosophy: it is more important to emphasize customers than competition in developing a successful business, or a successful business career. That is, it is more important to emphasize the cooperative nature of relationships than the competitive aspect. It is more important to emphasize the size of the pie rather than the division of the pie. A 50 percent share of a $1,000 pie is a better deal than 75 percent of a $600 pie. This principle has several important implications.

"We" Not "I"

In transacting, it is important to focus on "we," not on "I." That is, it is important to examine the gains to both parties to the transaction, not just your own benefits. This applies to all parts of the transaction. In seeking partners to transact with, seek those parties who have the most to gain by dealing with you. In negotiating terms of a transaction, seek those terms that will provide the greatest benefits to both parties, not just those terms most favorable to you. For example, if you can do some task more cheaply than the other party, then agree to do it.

The only area where there may be disagreement is on the price of the contract. The buyer wants a lower price, the seller a higher price. Because both parties gain from a transaction, there are joint gains, or a "surplus," to be divided, and the price term established how these gains are to be divided. But both parties have an interest in this surplus being as large as possible, so that they have the largest amount to be divided between them. They also have a joint interest in the deal being completed, so it does not pay to bargain so hard that the other party walks away. Of course, it is possible that there is no deal to be done (the buyer values the product at five dollars, the cost is six dollars), but it is important to be sure that there is no possible deal before walking away. It is not useful to break off a negotiation because one or both parties are trying to engross too much of the gains.

This is where viewing a negotiation as competitive rather than cooperative can become harmful. If one or both parties have a competitive mind-set ("Who does he think he is? I won't let him get away with that.") then the negotiation may break down, even though it would be in the interest of both parties for the deal to be completed. This is why it is important to keep in mind that the deal is cooperative, not competitive, and that both parties are going to gain from a successful negotiation.

One term that may not be obvious but that can be helpful is to be willing to penalize yourself. This is because penalizing yourself is a way of demonstrating a commitment to the deal and may make the other party more willing to do business with you, or to accept a better price from you. Such clauses are common in construction contracts, where the performing party will promise to have the building built by a certain date or pay a penalty for late performance. But what is not obvious is that both parties benefit from this clause—it is not a one-sided benefit to the purchasing party. Indeed, the performing party may even find it in his or her interest to accept a larger penalty in order to better promise commitment and so get the business. Another example is again from Amazon. Amazon keeps a record of things you have ordered and will tell you if something is a reorder. This might seem to harm the firm as it will reduce sales. However, since customers know that they will be warned if they try to repurchase something, they are more likely to purchase from Amazon in the first place. I have heard someone say, "I feel guilty if I buy a book from someone else because I may buy it twice." I myself have several duplicate books on my shelf because I did not buy them from Amazon.

Moreover, even though it pays to negotiate over price, it may not pay to negotiate the most favorable price possible. If you hope to continue to do business with your trading partner, then you want it to be in his or her interest do continue to do business with you. If you negotiate a price that gives all the surplus of the deal to you, then your partner has no incentive to continue to do business with you. Thus, it often pays to "leave some money on the table" in order to create an incentive for future business. Such an agreement is called a "self-enforcing agreement," and can continue indefinitely without relying on the court system for enforcement.

Ubiquity of Competition

There is another sense in which it is improper to characterize a capitalist market economy as "competitive." Such a characterization implies that other economies are not competitive. In fact, all economies are at some level competitive. The only difference is the dimensions over which competition occurs.

Consider a communist economy. Supposedly, such an economy "produces for use, not for profit," another meaningless slogan. Supporters of this sort of economy claim that such an economy involves cooperation, not competition. However, individuals themselves compete for advancement in these economies. They do not compete by making profits, as in a market economy. Instead, competition is political. The way to advance in a communist economy is to please higher-level officials. That is, competition is political, not economic, but it is real and fierce. Indeed, in the Stalinist era, losers were often shot or exiled to Siberia rather than bankrupted, so that competition was much fiercer than in a market economy. More generally, communist economies do not do very well at satisfying consumer wants, or even at learning what those wants are. This is in part because there is no reward for doing so and so no incentive to provide benefits to consumers.

In hunter-gatherer economies, there is also competition. Hunters compete to be the most successful hunter, and this hunter is rewarded, often with increased access to women.

So if competition is ubiquitous, how does a market economy differ from others? Fundamentally, a market economy is the only economy in which rewards accrue from satisfying consumer preferences. That is, participants in a market economy are rewarded for cooperating with consumers by providing the goods and services that consumers demand. It is in this sense that a market economy is cooperative and also in this sense that a market economy does the best job of benefiting consumers.

CHAPTER 6

CONCLUSIONS

The main conclusions of this book are that we should look for much more cooperation in the economy than we normally would, and much less competition. The economy is fundamentally an engine for cooperation. Competition is a secondary factor, and what competition exists is basically competition for the right to cooperate. We can apply this insight to many areas that are traditionally viewed as competitive or adversarial.

Imports

We traditionally view imported goods as competing with domestically produced goods. We view foreign producers as competing with domestic producers. Companies will advertise that they carry American-made goods, and consumers might pay more for such goods, or at least feel guilty when buying imported goods. And, of course, producers—firms and workers, through their unions—will use these feelings to lobby for higher tariffs and other barriers to free international trade.

All of this is based on a view of imports as competitors. This is, of course, the correct view if we take the perspective of the import-competing domestic firm. But there is no reason to take that viewpoint. The purpose of an economy is to maximize consumer welfare. If we take the viewpoint of the consumer, then foreign producers are just another source of potential cooperators. A sensible consumer will cooperate with (buy from) the entity that offers the best terms, whether domestic or foreign. If the foreign producer can offer a better deal, that means the resources controlled by the domestic producer—labor and capital—could be more productively employed elsewhere. Of course, some individuals (workers and owners of some capital) will lose from imports, but economists have known that forever. But it is well known that, overall, the gains to those who gain from imports (mainly consumers) are larger than the losses of those who lose.

Indeed, in policy discussions and in trade negotiations, we generally get the story exactly backward. The U.S., for example, will want to protect its own industry and to be allowed to export to other countries. Those countries in turn will want to protect their domestic industries and export to the U.S. So we view exports as the gain and imports as the cost. In fact, the gain from trade to the U.S. is the stuff we import; the cost is the stuff we must export to other countries in return. When the Chinese sell us stuff and accept in return pieces of green paper that may never be redeemed or may be redeemed at a discount because of inflation, then we are unambiguously gaining and they are unambiguously losing. That is because American consumers have more stuff (shirts, toys, TVs, computers, phones) to consume and Chinese consumers have less. If the Chinese want to subsidize firms that export to the U.S. (a dumb policy for them), we should certainly let them. The politics of trade is mercantilist, a system that has been discredited since at least 1776, with the publication of *Wealth of Nations*.

The politics of protectionism is well understood. Consumers gain from imports, but each consumer gains only a small amount and may well not understand these gains. (My shirts from China are cheaper than they would be if they were made in the U.S., but I have no idea how much cheaper.) On the other hand, firms and workers in the import-competing industry lose substantial amounts and are fully aware that they are losing. Public choice theory teaches that in these circumstances the political process will often work in favor of the concentrated group.

There are major federal programs that attempt to determine if foreigners are selling goods to the U.S. market at a lower price than they are selling in their own market. If so, then the foreign firm is penalized. This is a remarkably stupid policy. First of all, in general there is no reason why foreign producers would sell to the U.S. at a lower price, although in some circumstances "price discrimination" in our favor (lower U.S. prices) might be profitable for them. More importantly, however, is that the policy is exactly backward. If foreigners for some reason want to offer us goods at a discount, the proper response is gratitude. If we can buy stuff cheaper from them than can their own citizens, their citizens might correctly be upset, but we should be grateful. We are simply cooperating on more favorable terms, and this is in our interest.

The task of lobbyists trying to gain protection from imports is made easier by the language that is used. We refer to imports competing with domestic producers and often to "trade wars." If we stressed the cooperative nature of trade and the cooperation that is involved, then lobbyists would still seek protection, but they would at least have a more difficult time.

There is now a movement to reduce cooperation further by purchasing only locally grown food—being a "locavore." The theory behind this is apparently that locally grown food will require less energy in transportation. But if the price of nonlocal food includes the cost of transportation and is still a better buy (cheaper, or better in timing or quality), then a rational consumer will buy the nonlocal food.

There is no point in eliminating cooperation with all food producers except those in your own small area. Our ancestors lived this way
because they had no choice, but we do have choices, which makes us
better off.

Immigrants

A similar analysis applies to immigrants. We sometimes view immigrants as competing with American workers for jobs. For some small
subset of American workers, this might be correct. But overall, immigrants are simply another source of people for us to cooperate with.
It is easy to show that average income for U.S. citizens increases if we
allow more immigration.

Immigration has another benefit. It is well-known that the age
distribution in the U.S. (as in much of the developed world) is becoming
older, which is going to create real problems for Social Security, Medicare, and other age-related programs. This is because there may not be
enough young workers to support the old, retired workers. Moreover,
young workers are often more productive and more creative than old
workers. The solution is, of course, more immigrants. Immigrants are
a great deal for us. Some other country bears the cost of supporting
young people until they become old enough to work and earn, then
they come here and we get the benefit of that investment.

Fortunately, the U.S. is still productive enough and free enough
and rich enough so that skilled people from all over the world want to
come here. We are remarkably foolish not to let them. We now have
scientists and engineers graduating with bachelor's or even doctoral
degrees from American universities, and then we make them leave.
This is utter stupidity: the smartest people from all over the world
want to come here, and we don't let them.

I don't want to be accused of being hypocritical. In my own field of
economics, immigrants are now a majority of new doctorates. Earlier,
American economics was greatly enriched by a wave of immigrants

from Europe fleeing the Nazis. It might appear that American-born economists are in competition with these economists. However, the relationships are much more cooperative than competitive. In my own department, I have or have had colleagues from India, China, Bangladesh, Germany, Italy, Russia, the Ukraine, Korea, Bolivia, Japan, Iran, and Canada, and I have written papers (cooperated) with a half dozen of them. It is not clear that we could even offer a major without foreign-born economists. The field of economics would be much poorer without the contributions of immigrant economists. We economists would have much less material to teach, and our research would be impoverished as well. My subfield, law and economics, was initially created by Nobel laureate Ronald Coase, an Englishman who spent his career at the University of Chicago. It is not clear what my career would have looked like without the work of Professor Coase and other immigrant economists.

More generally, immigrants are a source of labor cooperating with American labor and capital and enriching us. One of the easiest ways to increase economic productivity and growth would be to legalize the immigrants who are here (with or without citizenship, a political, not economic, issue) and allow many more immigrants, with particular emphasis on educated and productive people.

Of course, there is a political aspect to immigration as well as an economic aspect. From an economic viewpoint, immigration is useful, but immigrants who become citizens also become voters, and we may justly be concerned with how such people are likely to vote.

Firms and Workers

It might appear that firms and workers are in conflict. Of course, there is one area of conflict: price. Workers want higher salaries, and firms want to pay lower salaries. But except for this ubiquitous conflict, workers and firms are generally cooperative. Firms cannot produce without workers, and workers cannot earn a living without a firm to hire them.

Much of the belief that there is conflict between firms and workers (or between capital and labor) is a remnant of Marxism. In Marx's view, firms exploited workers and forced wages down to subsistence. But this theory was based on the assumption that all owners of capital could collude among themselves to force wages down. In fact, such large-scale collusion is impossible. Any firm that cheated on an agreement to lower wages could hire the best workers. All firms would have the same incentive to cheat. Any collusion of hundreds of firms would quickly collapse.

There may be some issues where there is disagreement between firms and unions, ostensibly representing workers, mainly dealing with work rules. For example, unions might want strict seniority rules because a majority of members would favor such rules. Managers would want more flexibility in hiring and promotion because this would increase productivity.

In recent years, the percentage of the private sector labor force which is unionized has been shrinking rapidly in the U.S., from 17 percent of the private sector labor force in 1983 to 6.6 percent today. This may be because of the inherent low productivity of unionized labor forces. Employers are able to pay more to more productive workforces, and by eliminating inefficient rules governing workplaces, employers may have been able to convince workers to forgo unionization. In many jurisdictions, unions have won legal protection. Moreover, unions are still important for government workers, with 36 percent of the government labor force unionized. Here, however, efficiency is less important than in the private sector. Indeed, since union members are also voters, there may sometimes be a positive payoff from inefficiency, in the sense of having more workers than are needed who can then vote for the administration that hired them.

Firms and Customers

A similar analysis applies to the relationship between firms and customers. It might appear that firms and customers want different things. However, except for price (consumers want low prices, firms want high prices) they should agree. If customers want some characteristic of a good, as long as they are willing to pay at least as much as it costs, then firms should be happy to supply it. If some firm is not willing or able to make the product that consumers want, then forces of competition will lead some other firm to do so. A moment's thought should tell us that the huge variety of goods and services available to us is the result of firms making more and more variants of products, as consumers desire them. Views such as those of Ralph Nader and his followers that see firms and consumers as fundamental rivals are completely misguided and can cause much harm.

Government and Coercion

I have been arguing that voluntary agreements mean cooperation. However, government can coerce people into involuntary transactions. Government can also forbid some voluntary transactions that people might desire. The general presumption that voluntary transactions are cooperative fails when transactions are involuntary.

As I write this, Obamacare (the Affordable Care Act), which is revolutionizing medical care in the U.S., is a good illustration of both points. The initial version of this law both outlawed many voluntary transactions by requiring certain characteristics of all medical insurance plans and forced many involuntary transaction. That is, the law required that all health insurance policies have certain provisions, and all policies without these provisions are now illegal. Since many people voluntarily purchased such policies when they had a chance, it is clear that Obamacare has forbidden many voluntary transactions. Moreover, it made many other voluntary transactions much more expensive. For example, if an employer hires a worker for more than thirty hours per week, then the employer is forced to purchase health insurance for that worker or pay a penalty. As a result, many employers are reducing their hiring of full-time (forty-hour) workers and substituting part-time workers.

At the same time, Obamacare initially forced many people to either purchase insurance (which they may not want) or pay a penalty, although this provision has been repealed. This is forcing a transaction which may not be voluntary and therefore may not be cooperative.

Obamacare is extreme in that it is very unpopular with many citizens. However, its nature is not different from other government policies which often force involuntary transactions and forbid voluntary transactions (although, unlike Obamacare, in most cases the requirements and the bans are separate actions). Some examples of forbidden cooperative transactions: It is illegal to purchase pharmaceuticals which have not been approved by the Food and Drug Administration. It is illegal to work for less than the government-mandated minimum wage. It is illegal to purchase many drugs. It is illegal in most jurisdictions to purchase or sell sexual services and gambling services. In many jurisdictions, it is illegal to purchase services from unlicensed practitioners of many professions (medical, legal, and many other categories). It is sometimes illegal to hire certain immigrant workers. It is also illegal to purchase some goods made in other countries without paying a penalty (called a "tariff").

Coerced transactions are less common. However, taxation is a coerced payment to the government. For some services, these coerced payments actually facilitate cooperation, as for public goods. (Public goods are goods that citizens want, such as national defense, but are unable to voluntarily pay for because of free rider problems.) However, for many other goods, citizens are coerced into paying even though they would prefer that the good not be purchased. In the past, some citizens were forced to accept employment in the military (a draft) even if they did not want that job. Some farmers are forced to sell their crops to the government or to a cooperative even if they would prefer not to. The argument that voluntary transactions are cooperative and value-increasing, of course, does not apply to involuntary transactions.

Inequality and the Morality of Markets

Markets are often viewed as immoral, in part because they generate wide levels of inequality. Some people are extremely wealthy, while others would starve without some sort of assistance, either private or governmental. If we view the economy as competitive and focus on the competitors of the wealthy, then we might say that the rich are "ruthless" or "cutthroat" competitors and have become rich by attacking and beating their rivals.

But what does it mean to be a fierce competitor? Generally, it means cutting prices and undercutting competitors. From the viewpoint of the competitors, this is immoral and harmful behavior. But put on the cooperative lens. Undercutting prices is just a way to better cooperate with purchasers. A ruthless competitor offers a better deal to customers. From the cooperative viewpoint, being a strong competitor is a highly moral act because it provides goods and services to consumers at the lowest possible price.

How about the really rich and the really poor? The rich are easy: As we have seen many times throughout this book, being rich just means that you have done a very good job of cooperating with consumers and others, and have provided goods and services to them at the lowest price. The poor are poor basically because they have nothing to offer to others. This is a sad position, but it was not created by the market. In fact, by generating more income for society, a market economy can devote more resources to these people, through either private charity or through government transfers. A market economy also allows for investment in human capital, so that there will be fewer people with no valuable skills to offer for sale.

Racism, Genocide, and Other Horribles

Although this book deals with economics, some of the greatest costs of confusing cooperation with competition are outside the realm of economics. Because we view ourselves as competing with other workers, we may take steps to harm them or even to kill them. Racism is aimed at reducing competition from workers of another race. Sexism is aimed at reducing competition from women. Genocide is aimed at eliminating an entire population of "competitors." If we understood that most economic relationships are cooperative rather than competitive, then we might feel less hostility toward others, and realize that another group may have a comparative advantage in some activity and that therefore we could all gain from increased cooperation.

In Conclusion: What Should Economists Do?

As a final note, I want to suggest that this book has a lesson for economists in explaining what we should do to try to win understanding of our ideas by policymakers and the public. Bryan Caplan (2008) has shown that public understanding of economic issues is flawed, and Jim Kau and I (Kau and Rubin, 1979) have shown that these beliefs drive actual policy outcomes. We economists commonly make suggestions to policymakers about desirable policies, but my suggestions here are for economists themselves.

If we understand the biases that people untrained in economics bring with them, then we can be more effective in explaining our positions. For example, in discussing taxes, we economists emphasize the efficiency of different tax schemes. But to the untrained citizen, the issue is the burden of the tax and its "fairness." This is because of the zero-sum nature of much thinking. We might begin our analysis one step further back and first point out that different tax schemes have implications for the size of the pie, before explaining how some are more efficient than others. In discussing international trade and immigration, zero-sum thinking leads citizens to focus on jobs. Again, we should understand the source of this bias and explain how these policies lead to larger incomes in general. In discussing market regulation, we might point out that each regulation impacts both sides of a market—if an employer cannot pay less than the minimum wage, than a worker cannot accept a job paying less. We might also spend more time discussing the process nature of economic activities and explain that motives are less important than outcomes.

In communicating with noneconomists, we should emphasize the cooperative nature of the economy. For example, we should pay much more attention to cooperation and gains from trade in our textbooks. We write op-eds and economists often appear on TV. In those contexts, as well, we could pay more attention to cooperation. If someone says that "Amazon (or Walmart) is driving small firms out of business" we could point out that they are doing so by doing a better job of cooperating with consumers, and that consumers are made better off by this improved cooperation. In general, if we change out thinking to focus on the cooperative aspect of economic interactions, we can better inform our listeners and convince others of the benefits of markets.

We could also provide real benefits to our students if we teach them the cooperative nature of markets. In part because of our emphasis on competition, students often enter the labor market believing that they must compete with others for promotions and success. In fact, if they learn to cooperate with customers and with superiors and subordinates, they can advance their careers more quickly. Other students may avoid business as a career because they think of it as being overly competitive. Understanding the cooperative nature of markets may lead some to happier and more successful and productive careers.

The most important thing we can do is continually point out that the world is not zero-sum, and that the free capitalist economy is the largest cooperative system in the world.

BIBLIOGRAPHY

Becker, G. S. (1964). *Human capital*. New York, NY: Columbia University Press.

Bernstein, Lisa (1992). Opting out of the legal system: Extralegal contractual relations in the diamond industry. *Journal of Legal Studies, 21*(1), 115–157.

Betzig, L. (1986). *Despotism and differential reproduction: A Darwinian view of history*. New York, NY: Aldine de Gruyter.

Boyer, Pascal, and Michael Bang Petersen (2018). "Folk-Economic Beliefs: An Evolutionary Cognitive Model." *Behavioral and Brain Sciences, 41*. Available online.

Brooks, A. C. (2010). *The battle: How the fight between free enterprise and big government will shape America's future*. New York, NY: Basic Books.

Buchanan, J. (1964). "What should economists do?" *Southern Economic Journal, 30*(3), 213–222.

Caplan, B. (2008). *The myth of the rational voter: why democracies choose bad policies*. Princeton, NJ: Princeton University Press.

Clark, J. R., and D. R. Lee (2011). "Markets and morality." *Cato Journal, 31*(1), 1–1–26.

Colvin, J. (2017, October 2). "Trump advisers insist tax cut proposal won't favor the rich." Associated Press, *Sarasota Herald-Tribune*, 2.

Council for Economic Education (2007). "Test of understanding in college economics." *Microeconomics* (4th ed.).

Courtois, Stéphane (2017). *The Black Book of Communism*, Blue Edition.

Friedman, M. (1962). *Capitalism and freedom*. Chicago: University of Chicago Press.

Friedman, Milton. (1972/1988). "Capitalism and the Jews." Address to the Mont Pelerin Society, 1972. Reprinted in *The Freeman*, 1988. Retrieved from http://www.fee.org/the_freeman/detail/capitalism-and-the-jews#axzz2a4cRX9eQ.

Geary, J. (2011). *I is an other: The secret life of metaphor and how it shapes the way we see the world*. New York, NY: HarperCollins Perennial.

Gwartney, J. D., and R. Lawson (2007). *Economic freedom of the world*. Vancouver, Canada: Fraser Institute.

Gwartney, J. D., R. A. Lawson, and W. Block (1996). *Economic freedom of the world*. Vancouver, Canada: The Fraser Institute.

Gowlett, J. (1992). "Tools: The paleolithic record." In S. Jones, R. Martin, D. Pilbeam, and S. Bunney (Eds.), *The Cambridge encyclopedia of human evolution*. New York, NY: Cambridge University Press.

Hayek, F. (1945). "The use of knowledge in society." *The American Economic Review* 35(5), 19–30.

Jones, C. I. (2001). "Was an industrial revolution inevitable? Economic growth over the very long run." *Advances in macroeconomics*.

Kahneman, D. (2011). *Thinking: Fast and slow*. New York, NY: Farrar, Straus and Giroux.

Kau, J. B., and P.H. Rubin (1979). "Self interest, ideology, and logrolling in congresional voting." *Journal of Law and Economics*, 22(2), 365–384.

Kleiner, M. M., & Krueger, A. B. (2010). The prevalence and effects of occupational licensing. *British Journal of Industrial Relations*.

Kling, Arnold (2016). *Specialization and trade*. Cato Institute, Washington, D.C.

Kotler, P., and G. Armstrong (2010). *Principles of marketing* (13th ed.). Upper Saddle River, NJ: Prentice-Hall.

Kremer, M. (1993). "Population growth and technological change: One million B.C. to 1990." *Quarterly Journal of Economics*, 108, 681–1–716.

Leiser, David, and Yhonatan Shemesh (2018). *How we misunderstand rconomics and why it matters*. London, England: Routledge.

Newport, Frank (2018). "Democrats More Positive About Socialism Than Capitalism." Gallup, August 13.

Nozick, R. (1977). *Anarchy, state, and utopia*. New York, NY: Basic Books.

Piketty, T., and E. (2003). "Income inequality in the United States, 1913–1998." *Quarterly Journal of Economics*, 118, 1–1–39.

Pinker, S. (2003). *The blank slate: The modern denial of human nature*. New York, NY: Penguin Books.

Pinker, S. (2011). *The better angels of our nature*. New York, NY: Penguin Books.

Pipes, D. (1999). *Conspiracy: How the paranoid style flourishes and where it comes from*. New York, NY: Touchstone.

Posner, R. (2014). *Economic analysis of law* (9th ed.). New York, NY: Aspen Publishers.

Rasmussen Report (2018). July 25, online.

Read, L. (1958). "I, pencil: My family tree as told to Leonard E. Read." December 1958 issue of *The Freeman*. Widely reprinted.

Ribstein, L. E. (2012). "Wall Street and Vine: Hollywood's view of business." *Managerial and Decision Economics*, 33(4), 211–1–248.

Rubin, P. H. (1990). *Managing business transactions*. New York, NY: Basic Books.

Rubin, P. H. (2002). *Darwinian politics: The evolutionary origin of freedom*. New Brunswick, NJ: Rutgers University Press.

Rubin, P. H. (2003). "Folk economics." *Southern Economic Journal*, 70(1), 157–171.

Rubin, P. H. (2014a). "Emporiophobia (fear of markets): Cooperation or competition?" *Southern Economic Journal*.

Rubin, P. H. (2014b). "Buchanan, economics and politics." *Southern Economic Journal*.

Rubin, Paul H., and J. Shepherd (2007). "Tort reform and accidental deaths." *Journal of Law and Economics*, 50(2), 221-1-238.

Schelling, T. C. (1978). *Micromotives and macrobehavior*. New York, NY: W. W. Norton and Company.

Schumpeter, J. A. (1942). *Capitalism, socialism and democracy*. New York, NY: Harper.

Shtulman, A. (2017). *Scienceblind: Why our intuitive theories about the world are so often wrong*. New York, NY: Basic Books.

Shugan, S. M. (2006). "Antibusiness movies and folk marketing." *Marketing Science*, 25(6), 681-685.

Smith, A., and B. Yandle (2014). *Bootleggers and Baptists: How economic forces and moral persuasion interact to shape regulatory policies*. Washington, DC: Cato Institute Press.

Sowell, T. (2011). *Intellectuals and society*. New York, NY: Basic Books.

Stigler, G. J. (1957). "Perfect competition, historically contemplated." *Journal of Political Economy*, 65(1), 1-17.

Sunstein, C. R., and A. Vermeule (2009). "Conspiracy theories: Causes and cures." *The Journal of Political Philosophy*, 17(2), 202-227.

Telser, L. G. (1980). "A theory of self-enforcing agreements." *The Journal of Business*, 53(1), 27-44.

U.S. Council of Economic Advisers (2018). *The Opportunity Costs of Socialism*.

Waldfogel, J. (1993). "The deadweight loss of Christmas." *The American Economic Review*, 83(5), 1328-1336.

YouGov (2016). *Generation Perceptions*, available online.

ACKNOWLEDGMENTS

Thanks to Bryan Caplan, Monica Capra, John Hamilton, Daniel Levy, Hugo Mialon, David Rose, Richard Sansing, and William Shughart for helpful comments on the articles which formed part of the basis for this book.

ABOUT THE AUTHOR

Paul H. Rubin is the Dobbs Professor of Economics Emeritus at Emory University. He has published eleven books, over one hundred articles, and numerous op-eds in *The Wall Street Journal* and elsewhere. He was President of the Southern Economic Association in 2012. He held several senior positions in the Reagan Administration.